Key Concepts in Psychoanalysis

Key Concepts in Psychoanalysis

STEPHEN FROSH

NEW YORK UNIVERSITY PRESS
Washington Square, New York

First published in the U.S.A. in 2003 by
New York University Press
Washington Square
New York, NY 10003
www.nyupress.org

The author asserts his moral right in the work.

Library of Congress Cataloging-in-Publication Data
Frosh, Stephen.
Key concepts in psychoanalysis/Stephen Frosh.
v. cm.
Includes bibliographical references.
Contents: 1. Unconscious—2. Repression—3. Defence—4. Projection
—5. Splitting—6. Phantasy—7. Identification—8. Oedipus complex
—9. Interpretation—10. Resistance—11. Transference
—12. Countertransference.
ISBN 0–8147–2728–X (alk. paper)—ISBN 0–8147–2729–8 (pbk.: alk. paper)
1. Psychoanalysis. I. Title
BF173.F898 2002
150.19′5—dc21   2002012090

Designed by Bob Elliott
Typeset by Hope Services (Abingdon) Ltd.
Printed in England by Biddles, Guildford

Contents

Introduction

OVER a hundred years since its origins in the work of Sigmund Freud, psychoanalysis continues to be a key source of insights and controversies across all the major disciplines of the human and social sciences. It is also a central element in Western culture's self-reflective process, used by individuals to make sense of their emotional states, by critics to comprehend cultural and political events, and by counsellors and psychotherapists to conceptualise their working activities. Whatever its virtues and defects as an approach to psychology and psychotherapy (about which there remains intense and active debate), psychoanalysis is thus a vital arena for people's ability to make sense of themselves and for scholarship; being literate in psychoanalytic concepts is nowadays a crucial component of cultural literacy.

The success of psychoanalysis in pervading everyday life is rather mysterious, in that it has the appearance of being an immensely sophisticated discipline with a highly developed structure of professional and theoretical activity. Training as a psychoanalyst or psychoanalytic psychotherapist is long and arduous – at least four years' work for people who are often already established in some related profession such as psychiatry or psychology, and involving between three and five sessions each week of personal psychotherapy for the entire duration of the training. Serious theoretical work in psychoanalysis is usually undertaken at postgraduate level, and the subtleties and obscurities of this theory, with its attendant specialist vocabulary, are enormous. On top of this, the truth-claims of psychoanalysis are controversial: not only do professional scientists and philosophers routinely challenge its claims to be scientific or even relatively well-grounded in fact, but non-specialists are often suspicious of it. Does the unconscious exist? Is talking about things helpful? Is psychotherapy just middle-class self-indulgence? In addition, there is a peculiarity of psychoanalysis, that it is rooted in the words and wisdom of Sigmund Freud, who died over sixty years ago and whose writings, while still evocative, show clearly the influence of his own formative period – essentially, the late nineteenth century. Why, then, should this difficult, demanding, out-dated, scientifically dubious, therapeutically inept, over-complex set of myths about human nature continue to exercise such drawing power, such cultural weight?

There are many powerful forces ranged against psychoanalysis. These forces include time limits imposed on psychotherapy by the economic realities of publically funded health care, the growth of alternative therapies such as family therapy and cognitive behaviour therapy which profess to be able to achieve greater (or at least speed-ier) effectiveness, and most significantly the explosion of interest and belief in biomedical treatments and their accompanying claims to be able to explain psychological phenomena on biochemical and genetic grounds. Without doubt these developments have forced psycho-analysis onto the defensive both in terms of therapeutic practice and as a system of 'scientific' knowledge, and the demise of psychoanalysis has consequently been announced many times. A simple and rather glib way out of this dire situation is to assert that the continuing cul-tural debate over psychoanalysis is itself part of the evidence that it is still alive: why keep flogging it if the horse is really already dead? It must mean something – perhaps even, as analysts have been rather too ready to say, it shows how afraid the critics of psychoanalysis are of the truth it actually holds. That is, the attacks on it are best under-stood, in psychoanalytic terms, as a defence against it. Well, there may be something in this, but the problem here is that if one accepts this argument no critique of psychoanalysis can ever be mounted; it becomes a matter of faith that it is right, or at least that it possesses sublime truths, and all assaults, whether actually rational or neurotic, are interpreted away rather than thought about. There has to be some way to assess whether psychoanalytic claims are valid or not, even if that assessment can only be provisional, otherwise psychoanalysis will wither and die.

This death has indeed happened in specific places at particular times, as the institutions of psychoanalysis have lost sight of their radical vision and become stiflingly conformist. However, what has kept psychoanalysis alive is another kind of transformation: as the cultural tensions under which people live have shifted, so have the dominant foci of interest, theoretical ideas, conceptual languages and therapeutic practices of psychoanalysis shifted in response. One way in which intellectual systems remain relevant is that they speak to people's actual concerns, offering stories, explanations, modes of enquiry and practice which are in tune with what is 'really going on', what people struggle with in their everyday lives. In this respect, despite its many arcane features and the controversies which surround it, psychoanalysis has succeeded both in maintaining its fundamental postulate – that the unconscious exists – and in reinventing itself to meet the changing needs of the times.

There is no doubt that the image of Freud is still important in this, as a kind of knowledgeable father-figure who saw through the surface of people to discover (some would say 'invent') a depth. There is something flattering about this discovery as well as disturbing: we are not just what we seem, even the simplest of us, but all have something else within, something secret out of which our desires emerge, something which, in the last resort, may make us unpredictably tricky and intense. It also means that we can never trust ourselves or anyone else, because everything that happens is available to alternative interpretations, so the paranoid vision that so many people have of the world can be shown to have at least some truth in it. That is, Freud acts as seer and judge, revealing to us our own complexity but also the embarrassing nature of our innermost desires.

Since Freud, a lot has happened, but this basic position that human psychology is complex and requires sophisticated *interpretation* to encompass that complexity, is one which has withstood these developments. It also embraces a strand of social thought in which culture is a rather thin and fragile veneer covering over a repressed and dangerous deep – an image particularly resonant of the revolutions which so characterised the first half of the twentieth century, when psychoanalysis was taking hold. Moreover, there is something else which again is often experienced as true: psychoanalysis, from Freud onwards, argues that within each person there is an area of strangeness or otherness with which it is difficult to come to terms, something which cannot be pinned down but which is always troubling. This has in it some potential consequences which could be termed 'progressive': because all people contain otherness as part of themselves, there is a chance of being responsive to the otherness of the real outsider, however different (on grounds, for example, of race or gender) they might seem. But it also explains some of the terror with which the modern consciousness is infused: the enemy is not just out there, but very much within.

Freud's basic ideas have proved appealing to people struggling to make sense of the intensely conflictual nature of their position in modern society. They have also had a profound impact on how people think of themselves; that is, they have served to create the phenomenon of the 'Freudian subject' just as much as they have named something which actually already existed. This can be seen in the many everyday ways in which Freudian thinking has entered into culture, from the manipulation of desires in consumerism and its associated public relations and advertising industries, to common sense understandings of what can happen in relationships – for example, that a man might act towards his wife as if she were his mother, or that childhood difficulties might influence later life events. Or the psychoanalytic vision can be found operating in simple 'lay psychological' notions such as that someone might be 'lying to herself', implicit in which is a view of the mind as split between an area which is self-aware and a hidden area in which the 'truth' might reside. It could even be argued that the basic Freudian idea that we do indeed routinely 'lie to ourselves' is one of the foundational premises of what pass for contemporary relationships.

It has all become much more complicated, of course, in the post-Freudian period. Especially since the second world war and the subsequent escalation in the pace of global communications, what seems to have become more problematic in the lives of Westerners at least is not so much the control of passions (though problems around these still abound), but the capacity to form satisfying and deep interpersonal relationships. On the whole nowadays, people do not go to therapy because they are plagued with unmanageable sexual desires, but more commonly because they do not feel 'real' or secure enough to make lasting dependent relationships, because everything seems superficial or they tire of their lovers too fast, because no-one, including themselves, feels right. In psychoanalytic psychotherapy as in some other models, this change in the psychopathology of everyday life has produced shifts in theory and practice towards a more interpersonal or, as it is now becoming known, *intersubjective* way of thinking; here, the term 'intersubjective' refers to a focus on the unconscious relationships people have with the 'objects' of their affections and hatreds, fundamentally meaning other people. A whole school of psychoanalytic thought called *object relations theory* has developed around the question of the ways in which our 'inner worlds' are forged in the crucible of early intense relationships with others (particularly, in this approach, the mother), with the British school of psychoanalysis, led by the followers of Melanie Klein (whose relationship with other modes of object relations theory is rather tense) pre-eminent.

These transitions in psychoanalytic theory have ensured its continuing viability in the contemporary cultural context. Without claiming that psychoanalysis is unique here (because biomedicine as well as other psychotherapies offer alternative 'myths to live by'), its recent focus on the very complex links between relationships with others and the 'intrapsychic' structures of people's minds has meant that it can indeed participate in the fervent debates on what makes a life worth living or capable of being lived. If people feel harassed by the conditions of their existence, they need languages which can offer them some leverage on this, explaining why and suggesting things that might be done. Psychoanalysis, not uniquely but nevertheless powerfully, has shaped itself to be able to do this, as through clinical and other modes of observation it has created a complex understanding of what relationships mean. How do we manage anxiety, including that created in us by other people? What can one do with hate and its intimate link with love? What sort of emotional containment does a person, a child, a patient, need in order to be able to develop some sense of self? How can we feel real in our contacts with others? These, paradigmatically, are key issues in the contemporary social world, and they are precisely what psychoanalysis in its object relational and Kleinian guises focuses upon.

Not everybody is keen on these developments, however, and there are certainly psychoanalysts who have stood out against the object relational move in order to continue to assert the radical vision of psychoanalysis as a discipline stressing the *otherness* to be found within each of us, the impossibility of ever being 'whole' or constructing a self in a satisfying way. In the past twenty-five years or so, it is the form of psychoanalysis originating with the French analyst Jacques Lacan which has provided a rallying point for many such resistors. This is because the Lacanian approach both demonstrates the workings of culture in forming the 'human subject' and asserts the continuing value of the psychoanalytic vision of something 'internal' which can never be tamed, which is not reducible to what has happened or what has been put 'into' it. Without labouring the technicalities of the theory here, the great contribution of Lacanian and some other related forms of psychoanalysis is to offer a theory of how the human subject becomes a part of culture, whilst also holding open the possibility of a practice which is based on the tackling of illusion. That is, in a social context in which it is sometimes easier to stop thinking and seek refuge in therapeutic certainties about human 'needs' and how they can be met, Lacanian psychoanalysis reminds us that our *desires* are endless, always seeking expression, always hoping for – and maybe deserving – more.

Developments in theory have been paralleled and to some extent driven by developments in therapeutic practice. The most obvious shift here has been towards a more intense engagement with the process of the therapeutic encounter, in which the analyst has increasingly been seen as intensely involved with her or his patient, at an unconscious as well as conscious level. For Freud, the analyst's task was as far as possible to see clearly what was going on in the patient and to help the patient see it too. With the advent of the more relational theoretical approach of the Kleinians in particular, the analytic concern has shifted towards the forging of a certain kind of emotional relationship – the transference – in which work can be done to ameliorate the intensity of unconscious conflicts in the 'here and now' of the therapy, drawing as much on the analyst's emotional responsiveness as on her or his intellectual understanding. That is, the idea that the truth of the patient can be 'known' from the outside in any straightforward manner has given way to a much more complex understanding of the interpersonal dynamics of the therapeutic situation, in which the analyst's unconscious is understood to be a participant. Again without treating this in any detail here, its importance is that it produces a vision of psychoanalysis as an impassioned and highly focused dialogue in which each participant becomes an 'object' in the mind of the other, infused with phantasy, but nevertheless cogent and real. Although people still seek in their analyst someone who might understand them clearly enough truly to help them, what they are more likely to find, all being well, is a person who is able to stay thoughtful in their presence, manage their anxiety and rage, and not be frightened away. It may be that, under cultural conditions in which people are more likely desperately to avoid each other's pain than desperately to seek it, this is a considerable thing to find.

Key Concepts

The argument here is that psychoanalysis continues to matter, both on a personal level to many people and generally in the culture as a whole. However, given the enormous breadth of contemporary psychoanalysis, the fervour with which it is contested and the detailed complexity (and often contradictoriness) of its conceptual and therapeutic system, it is very difficult to hold onto what it is about. This difficulty exists not just at the level of the theory as a whole, but at the very concrete level of the meaning of its vocabulary: when a psychoanalytic term is used, whether as a technical term or in everyday discourse, what does it actually mean? Is it being used in any of its various specific psychoanalytic meanings, or is it being appropriated to everyday speech and being used loosely? And what might be the relationship between these types of uses, what is added to common speech by the particularities of psychoanalytic understanding? Sorting this out is no easy matter, especially as the various languages of the various 'schools' of psychoanalysis have developed some autonomy from one another, so that important concepts such as 'splitting' or 'transference' can mean different things to different people. We have long been at the point, that is, where guides to psychoanalytic language are necessary.

This book is by no means the first such guide. There have been several 'dictionaries' of psychoanalytic concepts over the years, generally of high quality. Most of them have been written out of, or about, specific traditions within psychoanalysis: for example, Moore and Fine's edited *Psychoanalytic Terms and Concepts*[1] offers a fairly orthodox ego-psychology approach; Hinshelwood's *Dictionary of Kleinian Thought*[2] is an outstanding resource for understanding Kleinian theory; Evans' *Dictionary of Lacanian Psychoanalysis*[3] performs a similar function, perhaps slightly less successfully, for Lacan. The best and most renowned general dictionary (though influenced by Lacanianism) is Laplanche and Pontalis' wonderful *Language of Psycho-Analysis* first published in French in 1967 and in English in 1973.[4] An additional, much more selective introduction to some historically significant psychoanalytic concepts was produced by Sandler, Dare and Holder initially as a series of journal articles in the 1960s, then collected as *The Patient and the Analyst* in 1973.[5]

These various books are of great utility for practising psychoanalysts and scholars of psychoanalysis, but they also tend to be complex and too entrenched in the psychoanalytic movement itself to be easily accessible to general readers wishing to understand the use (and abuse) of analytic notions in personal and cultural life. On the other hand, general introductions to psychoanalysis, which abound, usually offer only brief statements of the meaning of some central concepts, often tendentiously or misleadingly described and almost always limited to the work of Freud himself. What is very difficult to find, is a reasonably sophisticated yet also introductory source for genuinely 'key concepts', those which most centrally encompass the psychoanalytic project. Providing such a source is the aim of this book.

[1] Moore, B. and Fine, B. (eds) (1990) *Psychoanalytic Terms and Concepts* New Haven: Yale University Press

[2] Hinshelwood, R. (1991) *A Dictionary of Kleinian Thought* London: Free Association Books

[3] Evans, D. (1996) *An Introductory Dictionary of Lacanian Psychoanalysis* London: Routledge

[4] Laplanche, J. and Pontalis, J.-B. (1973) *The Language of Psychoanalysis* London: Hogarth Press

[5] Sandler, J., Dare, C. and Holder, A. (1973) *The Patient and the Analyst* London: Maresfield Reprints, 1979

Which concepts, however, might genuinely be thought of as 'key'? As the existence of the dictionaries mentioned above attests, there are a huge number of concepts which have specific psychoanalytic meanings. However, at the core of the psychoanalytic vision are a very few axiomatic ideas. First and foremost amongst these is the claim that unconscious mental functioning occurs in each and every person, and that this unconscious activity is potentially disturbing to the person and is held in check by repressing and other defensive forces emanating from another part of the mind. Linked with this is a set of core therapeutic concepts, organised around the central notion that psychoanalysis is characterised by interpretive activity: if underneath the 'surface' there are hidden 'depths', then the task of the analyst is to find ways through to these, to naming and explaining the hidden unconscious material that lies at the source of a person's actions and hence is the cause of their trouble. What has become apparent over the course of the history of psychoanalysis, however, is that this 'naming and explaining procedure' is made even more complex and powerful than it might otherwise be by the nature of the relationship that springs up between analyst and analysand, a relationship full to the brim with phantasies, summarised generally under the headings of 'transference' and 'countertransference'

It is with these key concepts that this book deals in a series of short essays on the unconscious, repression and other defences and modes of mental functioning; and on interpretation, resistance, transference and countertransference. Other important terms mentioned but not dealt with in the essays are described briefly in the Glossary. The aim throughout is to be clear and accurate in the presentation of psychoanalytic ideas, drawing mainly on the Freudian and Kleinian traditions for the reasons given earlier, but also acknowledging the critical contribution of Lacanian thought where appropriate. A subsidiary aim is to show how these ideas might work in 'everyday life' – how, that is, they might contribute more fully to the ways in which we think of ourselves as personal and cultural beings.

Acknowledgement

Several of the essays in this book are based on arguments more fully developed in my earlier book, *The Politics of Psychoanalysis*, the second edition of which was published by Palgrave in 1999. Some of Chapter 9 ('Interpretation') is based on material from my book, *For and Against Psychoanalysis* (Routledge, 1997).

1 Unconscious

IF there is a single 'key concept' in psychoanalysis it is that of the unconscious. It is this notion that distinguishes psychoanalysis from all other approaches to human psychology, and it is also this notion that has infiltrated post-Freudian culture most completely. The unconscious is an elementary and inescapable fact of everyday life in the West; commonsense ideas such as that people might lie to themselves depend on having some basic appreciation of the existence of a mind which is split between a part about which one has knowledge, and another part which harbours secrets. Additionally, even in this simple example one can also see the workings of another psychoanalytic principle: that *someone else* might see the truth of a person's unconscious life more readily than the person her or himself. That is, I might realise that you are 'lying to yourself' more readily than you do; and the evidence for this might come from inconsistencies in your behaviour, such as incongruity between the way you say something and the content of what is said, or conflicts between your actions and your words, or even – and this is deep psychoanalytic water – because of something you make me feel, such as darkness on a cloudless day.

The notion of the unconscious gives us access to a way of seeing people and the cultures they create as endlessly inventive, with the option of regarding this as immensely creative or actively persecutory. On the one hand, we need not be limited by our capacity to order things in a rational way: the unconscious can speak for us, the 'it' inside us can have its say, and even the most prosaic individual may dream in verse. On the other hand, whom can you trust? People may say they love you, but inside be boiling with rage about which they are not even consciously aware. A person's motives are so deep, it seems, that one has to keep one's wits about one, interpreting endlessly, suspicious, finding meaning in even the slightest slip. The world according to Freud is thus genuinely one of illusion, in which (in line with many ancient traditions) what can be seen and heard all around is only a shadow, signifying the existence of something more material elsewhere.

What is this something? According to Freud, it is repressed desires usually of the sexual but sometimes of the deathly kind. According to other psychoanalysts, it may be destructive urges, linguistic constraints and/or representations of relationships long lost or never quite achieved. According to everyone, it is something disturbing and tripping-up; it is that which keeps putting stumbling-blocks in our path, which always disrupts the best-laid plans; that is, it is the source of every cliché we have about how we constantly make ourselves fail. Ernst Gellner tells the story of the unconscious as a cunning adversary, something which is always disruptive and always interfering with evidence. 'The Unconscious', he writes, 'is a kind of systematic interference, which hampers full and proper contact between the mind and its object, and thereby prevents effective knowledge'.[1] As a consequence, there is no data which can establish the truth of the unconscious, because the unconscious ruins the possibility of actual knowledge – it calls everything into question. Thus, although we can see the workings of the unconscious in everything we do, especially everything we do *wrong*, we cannot find the thing itself, the unconscious, because it always hides, it lives nowhere, and it blocks us as we try to know it directly. This even applies to psychoanalysts, even to Freud. Did he think he knew the meaning of dreams? That was only a wish, and as such a product of the unconscious itself; that is, the belief that one can understand the unconscious is in fact a phantasy.

What, then, is this 'unconscious', so brilliantly formulated as to pervade everything yet to be impossible to find? Freud defines it in terms of what happens when, in therapy, one becomes aware of the operations of resistances behind which lie impulses and wishes of which the patient seems to have no knowledge. More generally, it refers to the existence of ideas which are not just not being thought about (hence not just 'not in consciousness') but which are also radically *unavailable* to thought – they cannot be brought to awareness even if the

[1] Gellner, E. (1985) *The Psychoanalytic Movement* London: Paladin, p.83

person tries really hard, or at least it is more of a struggle than one person can manage on her or his own. These hidden ideas, however, have a profound influence on psychological life.

We have found – that is, we have been obliged to assume – that very powerful mental processes or ideas exist . . . which can produce all the effects in mental life that ordinary ideas do . . . though they themselves do not become conscious.[2]

Unconscious ideas carry out *work*, they make things happen, they are motivating. If we want to understand ourselves or others, we cannot do so without reference to the unconscious. Conceptually, Freud stresses the necessary connection between the unconscious and repression, defined broadly as a set of activities keeping disturbing ideas at bay: it is precisely the mark of the Freudian revision of theories of the mind that there cannot be one without the other. 'The repressed is the prototype of the unconscious for us', he states,[3] highlighting in this remark the radically new perception that is brought to bear by his particular theory of the unconscious. It is not so much that he recognised the existence of an area of mental functioning lying outside consciousness, for many thinkers, before and after Freud, have done this, and there can be little doubt that our mental contents are broader than that which we are actively conscious of at any given time. Freud's new contribution, and his legacy to us all through the impact of this weird and disturbing idea, lies in his detailed documentation of the way in which this area of hidden life is *primary* and *causal*; it makes us what we are.

The key idea here is that of the unconscious as a space of *dynamic* activity (which, incidentally, has given rise to the general soubriquet *psychodynamic* to refer to theories and therapies based on this idea). The unconscious is not a storehouse for unused thoughts, indeed, it is not a *place* at all. It refers, rather, to a type of idea, one which is hidden from awareness yet still active ('dynamic'), pushing for release. The importance of this claim is that it suggests that repressed material does not remain dormant in its unconscious state (the more everyday use

[2] Freud, S. (1923) The Ego and the Id. In S. Freud, *On Metapsychology* Harmondsworth: Penguin, 1984, p.352
[3] Ibid.

of the term 'unconscious', as in 'he is unconscious'), but has a life of its own, with its own build-ups and releases of tension. Freud notes that, if anything, unconscious material develops more energetically than material which is governed by conscious thought, which always has to take into account the constraints imposed by reality. However, this is not to say that what he calls the 'proliferation in the dark' demonstrated by unconscious material cannot be charted. The maps are obtained through the analysis of dreams and mistakes such as the famous 'Freudian slips' of the tongue, and from the symptoms of neuroses; these give rise to a vision of the unconscious as an entity in which all is wish, impulse and drive, where reality has no place and there are no constraints upon desire.

'There are in this system,' writes Freud, 'no negation, no doubt, no degrees of certainty.'[4] This negative description of the unconscious, as something which does not suffer from the limits placed upon it by the need to function adequately in the real world, is a critical component both of its dangerous seditiousness and its appeal to many who seek something else than that which is given to them. The unconscious dispenses with time, with the need to avoid contradiction, with reality itself; it is the primary negation, the opponent of the world of order and common-sense, the great revolutionary of everyday life. For conventional analysts, this can all get out of hand and require therapy – being overtaken by phantasy is not a recipe for successful survival in the world. On the other hand, if one seeks a Utopian alternative to the current human condition, the unconscious offers a certain kind of yardstick, in which desire rules. This might, of course be considered a rather infantile and anti-social Utopia, labouring under the command, 'Do as I wish!', but at least it is a reminder built into each of us that the familiar world need not be the only one. As Freud notes, if we look carefully at ourselves, we are compelled to recognise that we are subject to forces which might feel alien, the 'it' of the unconscious id – perhaps the source of those fantasies of being abducted by aliens which afflict so many people. Our actions are only explicable when we refer them to 'another site' than consciousness, when we renounce the

---

[4] Freud, S. (1915) The Unconscious. In S. Freud, *On Metapsychology* Harmondsworth: Penguin, 1984, p.190

claim that we have some special private knowledge available to us about our secret processes, when we treat our 'acts and manifestations' as if they belonged to someone else.

What, then, is the difference between conscious and unconscious material? Dynamically unconscious ideas have (i) been repressed, and are (ii) kept from consciousness by continuing pressure.[5] This distinguishes them from 'preconscious' ideas which are just what happen not to be thought about at any given moment – for example, where a car has been parked, or one's spouse's birthday (both of which might, of course, be actively and motivatedly forgotten under some circumstances, in which case they become genuinely unconscious – or, rather, the fact of having forgotten them masks a deeper repressed thought, presumably a hostile one). Precisely because unconscious ideas are repressed and thus are not available to conscious control, they give rise to behaviours and experiences which seem to come from 'somewhere else', for example statements and actions of the 'I didn't mean that' variety ('How could I have forgotten?'). So the concept of a *dynamic unconscious* is two fold: not only are unconscious ideas dynamic in the sense of having to be held back by an opposing force, but also in the sense of being *causal*. It is the unconscious that produces much of the warp and weft of psychic life, its richness and its confusion. *How* exactly this occurs is one of the mysteries to which psychoanalysis addresses itself; that is, how exactly do unconscious ideas break through the defences and achieve expression? For Freud, the main explanation was in terms of 'psychic energy': the emotional energy of repressed desire becomes split off from the conceptual part of that desire (the idea) and invested in something else – dreams or symptoms, for example. Hence the work of psychoanalysis is to find out what the unconscious idea is, uncover exactly why it is so disturbing that it cannot be represented in consciousness, and by doing so, draw its sting so it no longer has such power to cause pain. At that point, the energy which was attached to it and which, in a Newtonian way, has given rise to a more-or-less equal but opposite repressing energy (keeping the original idea out of consciousness), is released and made available for the development of the person's life. Freud,

---

[5] Wollheim, R. (1971) *Freud* London: Fontana, p.161

thinking of this as a process whereby the deep and threatening power of wild nature (the unconscious id) is harnessed and made directable by the person's ego, likened it to a 'work of culture' such as the draining of the Zuider Zee: an elemental force made available for human use.[6]

In this process of bringing unconscious material to consciousness, words are crucial. Freud argues that the difference between a conscious and an unconscious idea is that the former 'comprises the presentation of the thing plus the presentation of the word belonging to it, while the unconscious presentation is the presentation of the thing alone'.[7] That is, unconscious ideas are so slippery partly at least because they are not pinned down in language, but rather act in an unmediated 'thing-like' way. Once they are named, however, there is the possibility that they can brought into the light of consciousness; seeing them clearly in this way, having the words to control and express them, is precisely what makes them no longer unconscious. This emphasis on finding the right words to name what was unconscious and call it one's own, is why psychoanalysis is fairly dubbed 'the talking cure' and, it is claimed, is also the reason why, from time to time, psychotherapy might work.

The very radical nature of Freud's theory of the unconscious should now be apparent. First, it shows how the mind is *split*. In making behaviour comprehensible only through reference to a site other than consciousness, a site which is hidden yet still 'internal' to the person, Freud argues that behind the experience that we may have of ourselves as coherent psychological beings there exists a basic split in the psyche. We may think we choose what to say, select what to do (the 'we' here being our conscious, articulated selves), but in fact we are chosen, or at least our choices are constrained by forces which lie outside of conscious control or easy access. Secondly, Freud's description of the unconscious is an *explanatory* account, claiming to tell us what causes our behaviour and how and why these causes become hidden. Unconscious wishes are disturbing, so they are kept repressed; this

---

[6] Freud, S. (1933) *New Introductory Lectures on Psychoanalysis* Harmondsworth: Penguin, 1973

[7] Freud, S. (1915) The Unconscious. In S. Freud, *On Metapsychology* Harmondsworth: Penguin, 1984, p.207

means that they continue to operate, but are not controlled (or at least are not *fully* controlled) by the ego, which one can very loosely identify with what is commonly thought of as the 'self'. This in turn means that what we are taught to see as 'natural' in the human condition, the capacity to use *reason*, is only a small part of the story: behind every action is a wish, behind every thought an unreasonable desire. Psychoanalysis thus challenges the Western view that the distinguishing mark of humanity is reason and rationality, arguing instead that the human 'essence' lies in unacceptable and hence repressed impulses towards sexuality and aggression.

Although in the post-Freudian world different schools of psychoanalysis have gone rather different ways, the general idea of the existence of the dynamic unconscious is one point on which they are all in agreement. Indeed, the unconscious can in many ways be taken as a *sine qua non* for a psychoanalytic theory, marking it out from nonanalytic approaches (or at least those not based on Freud's theory of the unconscious). However, as one might have predicted, there is plenty of disagreement about the details: how the unconscious works, what it consists of, how it is structured. For example, does the unconscious contain biological 'drives' (or at least their representations) in the way that Freud thought, or is it better thought of as a space for representations of relationships? Is the unconscious primordial, containing the 'energy' for psychological development, or is it produced in response to frustration and loss (that is, through the effects of inadequate developmental settings) as a place where unmet wishes are housed? Is it in any sense 'real', or is it a metaphorical notion expressing the human incapacity to come to terms with disturbing or uncomfortable thoughts? Exactly what is repressed and does this vary from culture to culture and individual to individual, or was Freud right in thinking that in every instance the material which is repressed is predominantly sexual?

This is not the place to deal with all these issues[8] but only to note that many post-Freudian psychoanalysts have seen the unconscious rather differently from Freud. Particularly in the British 'object relations' tradition, the emphasis has been on unconscious *relational*

---

[8] See Frosh, S. (1999) *The Politics of Psychoanalysis* London: Macmillan (Palgrave)

structures, more-or-less built on the model of the earliest actual relations with important others, especially the mother. Hinshelwood,
writing from the standpoint of Kleinian psychoanalysis, comments,

The unconscious is structured like a small society. That is to say, it is a
mesh of relationships between objects. An unconscious phantasy is a
state of activity of one or more of these 'internal' object-relations.[9]

As it happens, Kleinians still find a large place for inborn drives when
considering the nature of unconscious life, but they also see it as elab-
orated enormously by the relational phantasies and experiences
which follow birth. For some writers, the unconscious does not even
exist until experiences of desire and frustration occur, requiring a split
in the mind to enable such trauma to be contained. But all psychoanalysts agree on one thing: that within each and every person there is
this arena of strangeness, of the out-of-control, outside-ourselves,
which constantly impinges on our lives.

[9] Hinshelwood, R. (1991) *A Dictionary of Kleinian Thought* London: Free Association
Books, p.467

2 Repression

THE notion of repression is widespread in ordinary conversation, betraying the mutual influence of contemporary culture and Freudian thought on one another. *Sexual* repression is the main shared idea: that some people are unable to act on their sexual desires is a more or less routine observation and is sometimes drawn upon as an explanation of many different sorts of psychological and social uptightness. Anger, aggression, religious enthusiasm; fundamentalism, intellectualism, political activism, feminism: all these and more have at times been seen – perhaps written off – as resulting from an inability to give voice to what is 'really' pushing for expression inside a person. In addition, the concept of repression can and has been generalised to apply to whole societies seen as preventing the expression of their citizens' desires, for example through 'repressive' state apparatuses that persecute those who challenge authority, or by other totalitarian controls. Here, while sexuality is usually one of the things policed, repression gains a wider scope, usually including the prevention of political activity of all non-conforming kinds.

One characteristic of these various uses of the term 'repression' is the idea that something powerful and energetic is being kept 'down', out of sight and unexpressed. Whether this process is an internal one at work within individuals, stopping them giving vent to their feelings, or external, such as the operations of the state, it is seen as *active*, requiring force. Without the exertion of this force, it is implied, the underlying impulses or desires – sexual or political – would burst through, disrupting the personal and/or social order. Repression can therefore be thought of as having two principal components. First, it is a work of *policing*, in which there is a scrutinising and repressing body (parts of the personality, institutions of the State) capable of spying out subversive elements and constraining their activities.

Secondly, it creates and is dependent upon the possibility of a certain kind of *splitting* between what is on the surface and what is underneath, in which the 'underneath', the repressed element, cannot be spoken of and possibly is not even known. In politics, those who represent 'the repressed' might well know this is their condition, but from the point of view of the social order, their demands are unrecognisable. For the individual, for example in therapy, acknowledging the reality of a terrain in which there exist repressed desires is half the battle towards expressing them.

The psychoanalytic concept of 'repression' is tighter than the version given above, but it also draws on and feeds the more common-language account. Included in it is the notion of dynamic activity on both sides of the repressive process: something that is repressed (which in much of his work Freud identified with the unconscious[1]) yet seeks to escape its bonds, and a repressing agent that keeps the repressed in its place. The nature of this 'repressing agent' shifted somewhat over the course of Freud's writing, particularly in relation to the gradual development of his understanding of the ego and the increasing complexity of his model of the mind. What is clear, however, is that repression is a term used in two distinct ways by Freud. First, it denotes a specific means by which unconscious material is kept out of awareness; hence, it is one of the *defence mechanisms* with the function of 'turning something away, and keeping it at a distance, from the conscious'.[2] Secondly, however, Freud used 'repression' as a general term for the mental processes that create and maintain the unconscious. This running together of a specific and a general meaning for the same term can create confusion, but it does also have legitimacy, in that the process of keeping disturbing material 'in the unconscious' 'constitutes one stage – to say the least – in many complex defensive processes'.[3] More broadly, once the workings of repression are fully described, it becomes apparent that all defences have a

[1] 'The repressed is the prototype of the unconscious for us' (Freud, S., 1923, The Ego and the Id. In S. Freud *On Metapsychology* Harmondsworth: Penguin, 1984, p.353)
[2] Freud, S. (1915) Repression. In S. Freud, *On Metapsychology* Harmondsworth: Penguin, 1984, p.147
[3] Laplanche, J. and Pontalis, J.-B. (1973) *The Language of Psychoanalysis* London: Hogarth Press, p.391

similar function, which is to keep unconscious impulses at bay. So, every defence involves repression, and repression in the general language sense is what every defence does.

Freud distinguishes between two types of repression.[4] The first is 'primal repression', which acts on the basic drives, or rather on their mental representations. What this refers to is the Freudian claim that there are fundamental drives, eventually theorised by Freud as 'life' and 'death' drives but always involving sexuality, built into the biological structure of the human being. These drives are represented in the mind by certain ideas or mental 'representations' which are so troubling to consciousness that they are repressed *before they are ever known*. That is, according to Freud there is an area of the mind which is always unconscious, with repression acting upon it from the start. Moreover, in the same way that policing can very easily extend its reach to take in 'subversives' increasingly far from the supposed centre of its concerns, other ideas which were initially not derivatives of the drives can become linked with what is primarily repressed, sucked into it and made unconscious itself. Freud writes,

It is a mistake to emphasize only the repulsion which operates from the direction of the conscious upon what is to be repressed; quite as important is the attraction exercised by what was primarily repressed upon everything with which it can establish a connection. [5]

The second type of repression is 'repression proper', which Freud refers to as an 'after-pressure', in which material which is available to consciousness *becomes* repressed because of the threat it poses to the personality. This notion of 'repression proper' makes it apparent that there must be some agency at work which does the repressing: it is not only that the already-repressed 'attracts' new material to it, but also that there are security police in the mind whose task it is to throw out disturbers of the peace. This system all became much clearer once Freud sorted out his theory of the structure of the mind, which in large part he managed in his book, *The Ego and the Id*.[6] What was most important

[4] Freud, S. (1915) Repression. In S. Freud, *On Metapsychology* Harmondsworth: Penguin, 1984

[5] Ibid., p.148

[6] Freud, S. (1923) The Ego and the Id. In S. Freud *On Metapsychology*, Harmondsworth: Penguin, 1984

here was a recognition that the 'ego', that part of our minds with which we are most closely associated – in German *das Ich*, the I – is both the element requiring protection from the disturbances of the unconscious and the origin of the repressing forces which keep these disturbances under control. That is, the security police exist within the borders of the country of the self, yet *nobody knows they are there*. Repression, like all the defence mechanisms, is an *unconscious* process; it derives its power in large part from the fact that its activities are so rarely exposed. Freud argues in this respect that the defences are housed in the ego, in part of the structure of the 'I' which is itself unconscious, and that it is from there that their war against the drives is mounted; and it is from there, too, that intolerable thoughts and experiences (trauma, for example) are thrown out, repressed, and added (unfortunately) to the armies of the night. This process is heightened by the existence of a third agency alongside the 'I' and the 'It' (the id, *das Es*, the home of unconscious drive impulses); known as the 'superego', that which operates over and above the ego (*das Über-Ich*, the 'over-I'), this agency is created out of the internalised aggressivity of the Oedipal phase and occupies itself in judgement and punishment over the individual's illicit wishes. Thus, more and more, the repressive apparatus congeals and coheres: our thoughts are subject to censorship, and we are, generally speaking, not even aware that this is the case.

The development of this theory, that the ego harbours its own unconscious repressive apparatus, brought about a significant change in Freud's thinking on anxiety, the central platform of his approach to psychopathology. Previous to 1926, and the publication of *Inhibitions, Symptoms and Anxiety*, his view was that anxiety is a product of repression, caused by the failure of the drives to achieve release. As such, it is a purely quantitative phenomenon, produced by undischarged excitation, the original lack of discharge being due either to a real interference with sexuality (the 'actual neuroses') or to early psychological events and repressions ('psychoneuroses'). This is a straightforward matter of psychic economics: because the drives cannot be expressed, there is a disturbing build-up of unreleased energy, and some of this is let off in the steam of anxiety. However, recognition of the presence of defences within the ego raised in a very forceful way the question of why the ego should have to ward off material arising from the id, of why repression is necessary at all. What would be the effect of subversion so feared by the ego? What would happen if these repressed impulses were allowed through to awareness? The answer given by Freud is that the ego is defending itself *against anxiety*. The *reason why* the repressed is so intolerable is that it threatens to overwhelm the ego's fragile man-oeuvres in the real world through the urgency of its fantastic demands; this creates anxiety in the ego and makes repression necessary. Thus, instead of anxiety being the result of repression, it is now revealed to be its source: 'It was anxiety which produced repression and not, as I form-erly believed, repression which produced anxiety'.[7] Anxiety no longer is thought to arise from repressed sexual energy; instead, the ego's anxiety sets repression going and is thus the primary cause of neurosis.

Repression is not always a smooth process, however, and because the pressure has to be kept up all the time, it is not always successful in preventing rebellion. Freud calls this 'the return of the repressed'; that is, the exiled material seeps through at times, perhaps when the garri-son is sleeping (in dreams), or its energy is sapped by distressing events (in neurosis, for example), or when the power of the repressed is just too great for the defences to manage (mistakes like slips of the tongue – Freudian slips – and the like). Sometimes the impact of this is relatively insignificant – there is, for example, sufficient censorship remaining in dreams to mean that little damage is usually done by them. But sometimes a crisis occurs, for example when the only way in which the tumultuous energy of unconscious life can be contained is to allow some of it expression in the form of neurotic symptoms. This can relieve the tension a bit, just as occasionally making promises or even concessions to the masses can make them sufficiently contented to pull back from outright revolution; but it also means that the ego is now fighting on two fronts. Previously, it was struggling against a dan-ger which in some fashion came from the demands of the drives and their associated material. Now, with the formation of the symptom, some of these demands are being expressed in a distorted but nonetheless disturbing fashion. The ego therefore has to turn its attention to a new struggle, against the symptom, while ensuring that

---

[7] Freud, S. (1926) Inhibitions, Symptoms and Anxiety. In S. Freud, *On Psychopathology* Harmondsworth: Penguin, 1979, p.263

the original impulses are not freed from repression. The way the ego attempts to manage this is by adapting to the symptom and becoming at one with it, that is, by investing in the symptom (learning to live with neurosis and resisting change, for example), whilst concurrently defending against renewal of the demands for satisfaction. The situation would only be eased by total success at repression, or by complete and uninhibited absorption in the unrealistic demands of the id – these states being not alternative means to mental health, but characteristic of either neurosis (ego sides with reality at the expense of desire) or psychosis (ego sides with desire and ignores reality) respectively. One of the pessimistic elements inherent in Freud's position is thus the avowal that there is no way that a balance can ever be fully achieved; nor can suffering of this form be permanently avoided or removed from the psyche. It is an inevitability, given our constitution and the structure of our minds, that wish will clash with reality, that the ego will have to fend off the demands of the unconscious and will hence have at times to restrict its power and acquiesce in the formation of symptoms. It is not just that the world is a hard and nasty place; it is also that the structures which give rise to anxiety and symptoms are permanent elements of the human mind.

Repression is thus seen by Freud as an active process holding disturbing, that is *anxiety-producing*, material in a state of 'being repressed', of being unconscious. The mechanisms of repression are themselves unconscious, acting from within the ego and superego to protect the core 'I' of the individual. One effect of repression is to institutionalise the split nature of the psyche; repression produces the unconscious; unconscious material is, broadly speaking, repressed. This model works clearly in everyday life and in social analyses, not just those produced by a variety of political and social theorists interested in psychoanalysis,[8] but more generally as an image of how a social order might work – an image based, as Freud's own social thought was, on the idea of an essential *opposition* between the needs or wishes of individuals and what society can tolerate.[9] That this is not necessarily

[8] See, for example, the influential account of 'surplus-repression' to be found in Herbert Marcuse's *Eros and Civilisation* Boston: Beacon Press, 1966

[9] Freud, S. (1930) Civilization and its Discontents. In S. Freud, *Civilisation, Society and Religion* Harmondsworth: Penguin, 1985

the most perspicacious or subtle rendering of the individual-social relationship is something which many social theorists have explored more recently, but it still has a strong hold over culture in general, and our reflections on ourselves in particular.

Numerous changes in the theory of repression have occurred in the post-Freudian period, as one would expect. Kleinians in particular have argued that repression is secondary to splitting, both developmentally and in terms of forcefulness. At the earliest stages, the argument goes,[10] splitting occurs between different unconscious impulses (loving and destructive); it is only later that a clear procedure of splitting conscious material from unconscious – that is, of repression – occurs. Consequently, whereas primitive splitting is characteristic of a mode of thinking which at the extreme is psychotic, repression does not threaten the stability of the self to any such great extent.

The more severe defence, splitting, divides the mind into two minds, as it were (object relationship and self in each part) with each separate relationship coexisting side by side (horizontally); whereas repression consigns part of the mind, now more integrated, to an unconscious realm without destroying the integrity (vertical division).[11]

This view makes a considerable difference to the theorisation of the 'split subject' of psychoanalysis, because it emphasises the precariousness of any integrity to which the ego might aspire; but it does not necessarily affect the way in which the image and theory of repression is taken up in the cultural domain. At the heart of all this is a notion that each one of us is always internally split; that as the repressed is created and denied expression in the process of this split so it also strives to 'return'; that in these returns can be found moments of great trouble but also of relief; and that the aspirations of people, whether as individuals or as social groups, will always be to some considerable degree at odds with what is possible. One hopes this is too pessimistic a view; but hopes are wishes and wishes have their unconscious components too.

---

[10] E.g. Klein, M. (1952) The Origins of Transference. In M. Klein, *Envy and Gratitude and Other Works* New York: Delta, 1975

[11] Hinshelwood, R. (1991) *A Dictionary of Kleinian Thought* London: Free Association Books, pp.417–8

3 Defence

T HE accusation of *defensiveness* levelled against others, perhaps particularly our loved ones, is one of the commonest strategies of argu-
mentation. Generally it denotes a supposed attempt by the other to
stave off an attack on her or his self, a process of denial, particularly of
uncomfortable emotional truths. In everyday use, this process is usually seen as relatively near consciousness – just pointing out the
defences should be sufficient for culprits to become aware of them,
although because of their investment in the denial, and the need to
preserve 'face' and self-esteem, they are very likely to continue in their
refusal of acknowledgement. The subtlety of all this should not be
underestimated. What is at stake is usually seen to be the stability and
standing of a self under threat from some external attack, usually
because this attack contains a personal accusation, for example a
justified grievance, an instance in which the 'defended subject' is or
has been at fault. In a way, defensiveness is often seen as directed
against guilt, and with it the need to apologise. The lay psychological
theory underpinning this is not necessarily psychoanalytic; it can just
as well be based on the idea of human subjectivity as geared to the
preservation of self-image and self-esteem, in which how we present
ourselves to others is the central problem of existence; a defence under
these circumstances might even be a straightforward lie.

There is, however, an alternative viewpoint here which leads a little
nearer to the psychoanalytic perspective on defensiveness and defence
mechanisms. In this version of the 'you are being defensive' accusation, what the person is seen as defending against is some inner awareness of an emotion or desire which they do not wish to acknowledge.
This emotion is something troubling or, more specifically, shameful,
to the *self*: for example the recognition that one is really depressed and
in need of help, or is deluding oneself with a fantasy of success, or

struggling with homosexual desires. Here, the possibility of 'defence' implies the existence of a split state of mind, with the uncomfortable emotion in one place, and consciousness and self-recognition in the other. Clearly, even though this image does not absolutely depend on the psychoanalytic idea of dynamically unconscious material held apart from consciousness, it is very close to it and very compatible with it.

What is key to the psychoanalytic notion of defence is this idea of protection against ourselves, that is, against unconscious knowledge and, of course, impulses. As with repression, which is both a specific defence and a way of designating the primary defensive operation of keeping something out of consciousness, the defence mechanisms are dedicated to preventing the disruption of the ego by powerfully seditious unconscious elements. 'Generally speaking, defence is *directed towards* internal excitation (instinct); in practice, its action is extended to whatever representations (memories, phantasies) this excitation is bound to; and to any situation that is unpleasurable for the ego as a result of its incompatibility with the individual's equilibrium and, to that extent, liable to spark off the excitation.'[1] As ever, psychoanalysis' vision is turned inwards, towards what wells up inside the individual; to the degree that external events – for instance, accusations – provoke defensive behaviour, it is because they spark off, or chime in with, unconscious thoughts. And as we know, unconscious thoughts are unconscious specifically because they are troublesome, because they are incompatible 'with the individual's equilibrium', because they unsettle the self. This may be, however, because unconscious impulses are incompatible with the realities of the outside world; that is, the individual may need to be defended against her or his own tendency to go to war with the necessary limits put on us by society. Thus, it is not always clear whether in the last resort the threat is from within or from without, an issue which in many respects divides some of the main schools of psychoanalysis.

In the reconceptualisation of the structure of the mind carried out by Freud in the 1920s, defence was made the task of the ego; that is, unconscious 'ego preservative' procedures operate in manifest ways to

---

[1] Laplanche, J. and Pontalis, J.-B. (1973) *The Language of Psychoanalysis* London: Hogarth Press, p.104

try to outflank the attempts by repressed unconscious material ('in' the id) to get through. The modes of operation of the defensive system – the defence *mechanisms* – were charted especially clearly by Anna Freud[2] and taken up by the (primarily American) school of psycho-analysis known as 'ego psychology'. For Anna Freud, what was most significant in analytic theory and practice was the balance between internal drives and external forces, leading her to focus on the unfold-ing of ego functions in relation to drive stages as a crucial develop-mental issue, and to explore the many different ways in which drives and their derivatives could be kept in their place. These mechanisms include repression, regression, reaction-formation, projection, intro-jection, sublimation, idealisation and (a particularly evocative defence for social theory) 'identification with the aggressor'; what they all have in common is that they represent ways in which uncon-scious material is either kept solidly out of sight (e.g. repression) or allowed through in ways which are seen as compatible with the demands of the social order (e.g. sublimation). The end point, there-fore, is a kind of peaceful coexistence marked from time to time by border incidents, with quick recourse to the police when these threaten to get out of control.

As noted above, other psychoanalysts have placed more emphasis on the inward-directedness of the defences, seeing this as a product of the threat derived from the drives themselves, irrespective of the atti-tude of the social world. The principal voice here is that of the Kleinians, whose vision is of a death drive acting from birth, which has dissolution and destruction as its primary function. Whereas the kind of defence mechanisms focused on by Anna Freud are aimed especially at controlling sexuality so that the individual behaves reasonably and correctly, the Kleinians argue that there are earlier, more 'primitive' defences the aim of which is to stop the personality collapsing under the terrorising power of the death drive. These defences – especially splitting, projection and projective identification – are sometimes known as 'psychotic' defences because they are produced as a response to the intense anxiety of dissolution provoked by the activities of the death drive, and because the ways in which they operate support a

---

[2] Freud, A. (1936) *The Ego and the Mechanisms of Defence* London: Hogarth Press, 1948

paranoid experience of the world that takes a considerable amount of undoing before the personality can begin to be integrated. What is central here, however, is the notion that the enemy lies *within*, not just because the external world is unsuited to our inner phantasies, but because these phantasies really are destructive.

Whatever one thinks of these somewhat different, even opposed, images of defence, there are some important lessons. First, because the defences are themselves largely unconscious, they often share the compulsive, intense character of other unconscious ideas; that is, one can be possessed by one's defences as much as by one's desires. The absolute refusal to compromise recognisable in obsessional defences is an example, as is the consistent projective activity of the individual haunted by aggressive or sexual feelings, or the philandering of the person unable to sustain intimacy. More speculatively, in the spirit of Klein, the splitting of the mind in the face of deathly impulses itself produces a paranoid sense of a persecutory environment bearing down on the person, potentially leading to destructive actual relationships which mimic a contorted inner world.

As will be seen from this, there is also a sense in which defences merge into *symptoms*, if the latter are understood as compromises between the impulse and what can be enacted, that is, between the repression and the repressed's return. Faced with anxiety produced by the pressure of unconscious wishes, the ego mobilises its defences; the more severe the anxiety, the more rigorously the defences will have to be used, which in turn gives rise to symptoms – ways in which the defences manage the wish, allowing the wish sufficient air in which to breathe without so much as to fill its wings. Thus, symptoms are to be understood as substitutes for something that has been held back by defences; as such, they are really instances of failed repression, themselves a 'return of the repressed'. Certain unconscious wishes have been defended against by the ego because of anxiety, but the defence has partially failed either because it has been inappropriately applied or because of the strength of the wish. The impulse finds a way through into expression by employment of a substitute that gets round the defence by mimicking it; this is what is meant by saying that the ego 'adapts' to its symptoms. Hence, the particular defences that are characteristically chosen by any individual will determine the kind of symptomatology that she or he is likely to show. For instance, repression (unconscious warding-off of sexual desires) is the distinctive character of hysteria, the original psychoanalytic neurosis, while regression (to anal certainties) and reaction-formation are associated with obsessive-compulsive neurosis. In consequence, the ego loses on two counts: it suffers because the unconscious wish is achieving partial expression, and it suffers because that expression is only partial. Neither source of suffering is escapable; in line with psychoanalysis' generally tragic vision of the human lot, the defences are always likely to fail.

It will be obvious that if defences and symptoms are so closely intertwined, then unravelling the defences will be a central element in psychoanalytic psychotherapy. Given the scenario above, what Freudians have been most concerned to do is to unpick defences so as to enable exploration of the unconscious wishes giving rise to the anxiety which the ego is seeking so compulsively to avoid. The idea is that articulation of these wishes in the context of the analytic encounter will strengthen the ego sufficiently so that less compulsive defences will subsequently be needed; that is, knowledge, or 'insight', brings (relative) peace. In classical psychoanalysis, the strategy by which this takes place is a gradual one. First comes a process of building up a working alliance with the patient, whose ego is led to side with the analyst by its desire for freedom from symptoms and by the support that the analyst provides. Initially, acceptance of the patient's defence may be a necessary strategy, but this is followed by interpretation of defensive activity that moves from surface to depth, from anxieties and impulses which are relatively near to consciousness to those which lie far beneath. The rationale behind this is that the analytic procedure can only be helpful if the ego can be protected against being flooded with anxiety generated by primitive impulses. This requires that defences are allowed to stay in place until the ego has been built up sufficiently to be able to cope with the anxiety of what lies beneath them; that is, the classical analytic procedure is based on a respect for the defences, an appreciation of the necessary function they have in preserving the integrity of the psyche. Only when it is clear that the defences are secure enough to manage, can the hidden feelings against which they are operating be brought to light.

While this approach might seem logical, with the analyst as a prop or support for the ego, it is not universally accepted, and here the Kleinians take issue with it. They argue that the only way to ease the pressure on the defences is to reduce the anxiety-producing power of the impulses against which they are directed, and this means facing up to the content of those impulses, however destructive and hate-filled they may be. Without facing the deepest anxieties head-on, they imply, the dismantling of defences will either allow them to pour through in a psychosis-inducing flood, or even more extreme defences will be brought into play, with perhaps much the same effect. Hence, Kleinians hold that interpretation of primitive unconscious contents and defences is crucial from the start of analysis; otherwise, the anxiety they generate will never be addressed, and patients will leave analysis with the unconscious 'knowledge' that their inner worlds are too disturbing for the analyst to deal with.

It is interesting to see how powerful images of floods and laboriously built (and carefully dismantled) dams are in all this. What this misses, however, is the idea that the defences are flexible and fast, constantly on guard and needing considerable creativity to outwit the rebellious insurgency of the unconscious. Kleinians, with their emphasis on envy and destructiveness, invoke a more terrifying image than do Freudians: without defences, we will collapse into psychosis. Not surprisingly, therefore, the defences they emphasise are more extreme or 'primitive' than those stressed by other psychoanalysts. But whatever stance one takes on this, it is clear that there is no celebration of the unconscious 'pure and simple' in psychoanalysis. Defences are *necessary*; the 'sea' which is the unconscious can never be completely tamed, nor will blocking it with dams ever fully succeed, for not only is it wild, but there are monsters in the deep.

4 Projection

THERE is a common, everyday experience acknowledged by most people. This involves being in the presence of someone who seems reasonably normal, calm even, yet feeling anxious and agitated oneself. Sometimes the presence of the calm other has a calming impact on the self, as if one's own agitation has been 'contained' by the other and made more manageable. Sometimes, the order of events seems to be the other way around: the calm other seems to have provoked the anxiety in the self, without losing her or his own appearance of ease. That is, a person might be feeling tense and realise that this tension 'actually' comes from the other, that it is being picked up 'unconsciously' and experienced as if it were one's own. In both examples, however, whether the source of the anxiety is the self and the other is a 'container' for it, or whether it is the other who is inserting anxiety into the self, there is an exchange of unconscious emotion going on, a process whereby a set of 'feelings' – or, at least, the unconscious ideas which give rise to them – are being scooped from one person into the experience of the other. Amongst the many interesting aspects of this phenomenon is the experience that the one who has 'lost' the feelings has genuinely done so; that is, the process of transfer of (for example) agitation is a clean one, leaving the original possessor of the feeling relatively free.

There is a second, more benevolent, experience which is also common, and which shows the other side of this mysterious 'scooping out and transferring' process. Imagine a mother with a pre-verbal baby. Without over-romanticising this image, one can envisage a mother who feels herself able to 'pick up', reasonably accurately, the emotions of this baby. So when the child cries, as she or he does, the mother might have to experiment a bit with how to appease the cries, but she might also feel 'inside herself', as a matter of 'intuition', that she knows what the baby is crying about (or for) – that she knows, for example, the difference between a cry of hunger and one of pain, of frustration or of miserable hurt. She might be wrong, of course, just as the individual who experiences what seems to be another person's anxiety might be misattributing it; but if she is right, even if this only happens sometimes, then something is being communicated without words from baby to mother, some intentional or at least emotional state, which is picked up and registered, somehow understood if not always consciously, and at the best of times responded to appropriately, with a feed, a comforting cuddle, or a calming word.

These relatively ordinary experiences are loosely collected together under the psychoanalytic rubric of 'projection' and 'projective identification'. The notion of projection began with Freud, but has been developed most forcefully by members of the Kleinian school of psychoanalysis, who have made of it both a theory of mind and a model of the psychotherapeutic process. For Freud, projection was a defence mechanism in which disturbing unconscious material is kept unconscious by experiencing it as if it belongs to another. So one's own aggression is denied and attributed to one's neighbour, one's lustful perversions are seen in others rather than oneself, and greed and exploitation exists everywhere except in the home. This is not just a matter of cognitive misattribution, in which a mistake is made about the actual origin of the misplaced feeling ('I thought I was anxious but now I know it's she'), but of something deeply unconscious; that is, as with the other defences, not only is the unconscious impulse in oneself not recognised, but the projective process itself is carried out unawares. The aggression or lust or whatever is felt actually to *be* in the other, and the strong sense of disgust one might then have at the other's supposed behaviour is rationalised as an ethical stance rather than a further unconscious defence. According to Freud, this process of expelling unwanted material is an aspect of the working of the pleasure principle: what is not wanted is got rid of, whilst what is wished for is 'introjected', taken in to become part of the self. Intriguingly, this 'taking in' counterpart of projection is elevated by Freud to something crucial in the building-up of the ego, a point to be returned to below; but overall, 'the Freudian usage of the term "projection" is . . . a clearly circumscribed one. It is always a matter of throwing out what one refuses either to *recognise* in oneself or to *be* oneself.'[1]

The process described by Freud, in which a feeling that properly belongs to the self is experienced as if it belongs to the other, is the simplest sense of projection, but it clearly does not capture the subtlety of the examples given earlier, in which something transpires between people in the form of a destructive or benevolent communication of unconscious states of mind. It is here that the Kleinian development flowers most fully. For Klein herself, projection and introjection were fundamental mental mechanisms out of which the ego develops. These mechanisms act cyclically to drag the mind from a state in which it is threatened with annihilation by its own destructive urges, to one in which a relatively stable set of internal structures exists and gives it a sense of permanence and coherence. What is key here, however, is that the material worked on by projection and introjection is not just unconscious ideas, but also *objects* – that is, internalised or phantasised people or parts of people (especially the breast), held in relationship with aspects of the ego.

Schematically, according to Kleinians, the developmental sequence is one in which the destructive energy of the death drive forces the infant's fragile ego defences into operation. As the infant's internal representation of the world is limited by her or his bodily experience to that of ingestion and expulsion, the defence mechanism available is itself built on that model; that is, projection, as the expulsion of unwanted psychic material, is a corollary of the infant's body schema, that things go in and out. So the destructive rage of the death drive is 'deflected'[2] outwards onto the available object, the breast, which has the dual effect of softening the internal world and making the external one more threatening.

The ego splits itself and projects that part of itself which contains the death instinct outwards into the original external object – the breast. Thus, the breast, which is felt to contain a great part of the infant's death instinct, is felt to be bad and threatening to the ego, giving rise to a feeling of persecution.

[1] Laplanche, J. and Pontalis, J.-B. (1973) *The Language of Psychoanalysis* London: Hogarth Press, p.354

[2] Segal, H. (1973) *Introduction to the Work of Melanie Klein* London: Hogarth Press, p.25

In that way, the original fear of the death instinct is changed into fear of a persecutor.[3]

At the same time as this catastrophe is occurring, the loving impulses of the infant are also projected, 'in order to create an object which will satisfy the ego's instinctive striving for the preservation of life',[4] thus making an ideal object out of the breast, in which hope is invested and which has the function of keeping love alive. The next move here is for the infant to take back in these projected impulses in a more integrated, tolerable way, something made possible only if the external world offers at least a modicum of safe 'containment', so that the destructive impulses are not experienced by the child as *actually* able to wreck everything. That is, if the mother (for the sake of Kleinian argument) is capable of withstanding the infant's aggression and responding patiently and lovingly to it, it becomes possible for the infant to introject the projected feelings, as inhabitants of loved and hated objects, and form gradually more integrated internal representations of them, producing a complex mind more capable of dealing with emotions and, especially, with ambivalence.

This is the general trajectory of development in Klein, theorised as the relationship between the 'paranoid schizoid' and 'depressive' phases; for present purposes, what is most compelling is the way in which it portrays a mind built out of the to and fro between internal, unconscious fears and desires, and the ministrations of the external world. There is, in reality, nothing which is purely inside or out, only an unending exchange, a transaction in which each is infused by the other. Although the urgency behind mental activity is pictured as deriving from inborn drive processes – the destructive urge and the anxiety to which it gives rise – the social world in which the child is embedded has a crucial function in modifying these drives and giving structure to the infant's mind. The mother, in her role as external object, is charged with the task of containing the child's bad feelings and translating them into new, more tolerable mental contents. It is her capacity to do this which allows the child to accept back the destructive urges which had previously been felt as terrifying and to begin to own them as part of an

---

[3] Segal, H. (1973) *Introduction to the Work of Melanie Klein* London: Hogarth Press, p.25
[4] Ibid.

integrated psyche. In post-Kleinian theory in particular, the structure of the mind is seen as created through this dialectical interchange in which the quality of the interpersonal encounter with the 'object' is a crucial counterweight to the strength of constitutional drives.

While the Kleinian version of projection communicates well the intensity of the experience of taking in and giving out that characterises the cycles of introjection and projection, it is with the notion of projective identification that the full force of the individual's immersion in her or his relationship with otherness can be felt. In this sense, psychoanalysis can be seen as a deep engagement with 'the other', and with the ways in which this 'other' is integral to the self. As mentioned earlier, some elements of this can be found in Freud, especially in the context of his work on melancholia[5] (understood, roughly speaking, as the taking in of an unacknowledged and hence unmournable lost object) and his notion that the ego itself is 'a precipitate of abandoned object cathexes and that it contains the history of these object choices',[6] that is, that the ego is built up in large part out of internalisations of otherness. (Cathexes are investments of psychic energy, a concept specific to Freud and psychoanalysis.) However, projective identification in the Kleinian sense is a further turn of the screw, and one intimately linked with the mechanisms of psychoanalytic psychotherapy as well as with developmental theory. This process, it should also be noted, links normal development, 'ordinary' unconscious communicational processes, and psychotic functioning within and outside therapy.

What is central to the concept of projective identification is the idea that it is not just feelings or emotions that are projected, but 'parts of the self', inserted into the external object both for protection and as an act of aggression. This is supposed to be a normal event in early development, occurring before there is any clear differentiation between self and object (or it would not be fully possible), but because of the persistence of infantile feelings and mental processes throughout life it operates just as noticeably and powerfully in adults, whether analytic patients or not. In its 'pure' form, projective identification appears to

[5] Freud, S. (1917) Mourning and Melancholia. In S. Freud, *On Metapsychology* Harmondsworth: Penguin, 1984

[6] Freud, S. (1923) The Ego and the Id. In S. Freud, *On Metapsychology* Harmondsworth: Penguin, 1984, p.368

be a negative procedure; it is defined by Laplanche and Pontalis as 'a mechanism revealed in phantasies in which the subject inserts his self – in whole or in part – into the object in order to harm, possess or control it'.[7] However, most post-Kleinian psychoanalysts have identified two alternative aims of projective identification, one more benign than the other. Hinshelwood states that one of these aims is 'to evacuate violently a painful state of mind leading to forcibly entering an object, in phantasy, for immediate relief, and often with the aim of an intimidating control of the object', while the other is 'to introduce into the object a state of mind, as a means of communicating with it about this mental state.'[8] These two 'aims' reflect the examples given at the start of this discussion, the former being a kind of aggressive attack in which parts of the self are put into the other as a way of relieving internal anxiety and mounting an envious assault, whilst the latter is a way of producing in the other a resonance, an unconscious understanding, which can form the basis of empathy.

As implied by its name, as well as being two alternative *aims* to projective identification, it also has two *components*: projection and identification with what has been projected. The projective component involves placing parts of the self into an external object either in order to deal with the anxiety these parts are producing (in the case of destructive elements) or (and here is the more ameliorating element of projective identification) so as to preserve something good and loving, to place it elsewhere for safekeeping. The second, 'identification' component of projective identification is the process whereby the person feels her or himself to remain in contact with those parts of the self that have been projected out, hence creating phantasies of control of the object by the self, or vice versa. Although there is always the risk, or experience, of being depleted by projecting valued aspects of the self into the other (which is one reason why feelings of gratitude might provoke associated envious emotions), this aspect of projective identification is a way of *communicating* rather than just dumping feared parts of the self. In psychoanalysis, it therefore enables contact

[7] Laplanche, J. and Pontalis, J.-B. (1973) *The Language of Psychoanalysis* London: Hogarth Press, p.356

[8] Hinshelwood, R. (1991) *A Dictionary of Kleinian Thought* London: Free Association Books, p.184

to be retained with the analyst's mind, conveying aspects of the patient's inner world and thereby influencing the analyst's emotional state. Conversely, it is the analyst's task to maintain a stance of 'reverie'[9] in which, like the mother, she or he can receive, tolerate and think about any projections received from the patient, however threatening, so as to draw some of their sting and allow them to be re-introjected by the patient in a more manageable, 'digested' form.

Along with Wilfred Bion, whose ideas are drawn on above, Herbert Rosenfeld is the Kleinian analyst who has written most systematically about projective identification.[10] Rosenfeld distinguishes between a small number of different kinds of projective identification, with differing forms and functions in the therapeutic situation. The major distinction, as before, is between 'projective identification used for communication with other objects and projective identification used for ridding the self of unwanted parts'. The former is obviously the more positive form: in infancy it is a normal mode of non-verbal communication with the mother, whose task it is to contain, mollify and restore the projected elements of the self so that they can be integrated into the infant's incipient ego. The analytic task in this situation is exactly the same. Psychotic patients project feared impulses and parts of the self into the analyst, who reduces their terror by surviving such 'attacks' without retaliating, and by making them intelligible through interpretation. Other forms of projective identification are less benevolent. When it is used for denial of psychic reality,

the patient splits off parts of his self in addition to impulses and anxieties and projects them into the analyst for the purpose of evacuating and emptying out the disturbing mental content which leads to a denial of psychic reality. As this type of patient primarily wants the analyst to condone the evacuation process and the denial of his problems, he often reacts to interpretations with violent resentment, as they are experienced as critical and frightening since the patient believes that unwanted, unbearable and meaningless mental content is pushed back into him by the analyst. [11]

[9] Bion, W. (1962) *Learning from Experience* London: Maresfield, p.36

[10] Rosenfeld, H. (1971) Contribution to the Psychopathology of Psychotic States: The Importance of Projective Identification in the Ego Structure and the Object Relations of the Psychotic Patient. In E. Spillius (ed) *Melanie Klein Today, Volume 1: Mainly Theory* London: Routledge, 1988

[11] Ibid, p.121

Rosenfeld describes a variant, but common, form of projective identification in which the patient attempts omnipotently to control the analyst through the projective process. Such a patient experiences her – or himself as having entered into the analyst; this means not only that the self-other boundary has been obscured, producing anxieties about the loss of self, but also that the patient phantasises the analyst as having been infected with her or his own madness. 'The analyst is then perceived as having become mad, which arouses extreme anxiety as the patient is afraid that the analyst will retaliate and force the madness back into the patient, depriving him entirely of his sanity.'[12] This is perhaps the worst type of projective identification, threatening the patient with disintegration, getting rid of the envious destructiveness in the mind at the expense of the mind itself. Little can remain here of optimism and hope, as the self flees from its fears into desperate fragments.

It can perhaps be seen that the notion of projection has been both stretched and thickened in this work. From a simple defensive manoeuvre of expelling unwanted material, it has come, particularly in the form of projective identification, to carry the burden of an explanatory theory of how development can occur, and also of how the process of therapy might be understood. Most interestingly, perhaps, it breaks down any severe notion of a clear separation between 'inner' and 'outer' worlds. Instead, we are treated to a picture of the mind always in dialogue, or perhaps in a *dialectic*, with otherness: what is inside comes from without, what seems out there is infused with bits of the self. This, as one might imagine, has been a fertile territory for explorations of such phenomena as racism, which has been explored psychoanalytically as a process in which hated aspects of the self are put into the loathed, racialised other.[13] However, it also holds within it the germs of a theory of more positive features of human culture, such as creativity, interdependence and potentially of sociality itself. Where the other is, so, it seems, are we.

[12] Rosenfeld, H. (1971) Contribution to the Psychopathology of Psychotic States: The Importance of Projective Identification in the Ego Structure and the Object Relations of the Psychotic Patient. In E. Spillius (ed) *Melanie Klein Today, Volume 1: Mainly Theory* London: Routledge, 1988, p.122

[13] e.g. Frosh, S. (1997) *For and Against Psychoanalysis* London: Routledge

5 Splitting

THERE is a sense in which the notion of splitting is at the heart of psychoanalysis. The most central perception, after all, is of a human 'subject' split between a conscious and unconscious area of the mind; as such, we can never conceive of ourselves as whole, but must always labour in the knowledge that something is acting or speaking from inside us, about which we have little knowledge and over which we have less control. For Freud, this is probably the crucial aspect of splitting, a term on which he otherwise placed less emphasis than he did, for example, 'repression'. The existence of an unconscious and of the repression out of which it is created establishes that humans are 'split subjects', divided between conscious and unconscious and also, according to the Freudian theory of the drives which make up much of the content of unconscious life, between sexuality and order (the 'ego preservative' drives of his first theory) or between the impulses of life and death. This is enough: from this point onwards there can be only the phantasy of an integrated psyche, never its actual achievement.

Freud might have been surprised at quite how central this image of a split subject has become to contemporary social theories, which offer a portrait of the mind in fragments and assert the impossibility of identity and its displacement by a contradictory and fluid selfhood punctuated only by fleeting moments of identification and stability. In current times, it is very hard to envision a return to any confident idea of the 'whole' self; at most, one can grasp onto the hope that people may struggle meaningfully towards integration as a kind of life project, knowing always (as Freud knew) that the existence of an unconscious means that this final state can never be absolutely attained. More commonly, however, there is either an awed and appalled recognition of the fragmentary nature of existence and the very partial possibilities for self-knowledge and self-elaboration; or there is a celebration of these very same things, an excitement at the possibilities which open up once one has decided to enjoy the ride. Freud would not have agreed with the latter attitude, but he might have had every sympathy with the former.

In psychoanalysis, there have been two important tendencies in developing the idea of splitting, one concerned with the way the mind forms itself out of passionate and opposed elements, the other concerned more with the fragmentation that occurs as the individual faces the world. The former is expressed most fully in the work of Melanie Klein and her followers. In this view, the essential components of the mind are opposed drives – those of life and death – the fundamental, biologically given and endlessly pumping activities of which give rise to a mental structure built around the relationship of split 'objects' (internalised, phantasised representations of external people and bodily parts) with split-off aspects of the ego. The task of life – of development, of psychotherapy – is to seek greater integration, whilst never losing sight of both the potential and danger of falling into more fragmentary states of being. More generally, although the main thrust of development is towards increasing the degree of integration of the ego, much of the verve and evocative power of the theory lies in its account of the opposite tendency, towards splitting and fragmentation. This, incidentally, is characteristic of Kleinian theory: despite its hankering after a therapeutic and 'reparative' stance, much of its poetic and emotional appeal derives from its unflinching encounter with negativity, with what always seems to go wrong.

Klein's account of how all this works is remarkable for its extreme nature and also for its theoretical fertility.[1] The newborn infant is at the mercy of its life and death drives, which are seen by Klein as present at birth, but there is also enough of an early ego to experience profound anxiety that the death drive will cause annihilation of its inner resources. This calls into play some powerful defences right from the start, these being projection and splitting. In a departure from the classical Freudian view, in which repression drives the formation of

[1] Klein, M. (1946) Notes on Some Schizoid Mechanisms; Klein, M. (1957) Envy and Gratitude. Both in M. Klein, *Envy and Gratitude and Other Works* New York: Delta, 1975

the unconscious and hence is the earliest real defence, Klein gives a key role to splitting, seeing it as a primitive way in which conflicts within the individual's mind (which, because of the ambivalent structure of the instincts, exist from the start) are managed. The argument here is that repression depends on the existence of a relatively strong ego capable of recognising and repelling unwanted material from consciousness, but splitting is 'simply' a matter of holding things apart, rather desperately most of the time, and can be achieved at the behest of an ego which is literally just coming into being, and struggling for continued existence. Thus, Kleinians argue that the passionate and perpetually conflictual nature of the inborn drives (life and death) generates anxiety which in turn leads to immediate and inevitable splits in the infantile mind. Psychic unity is not just empirically unobtainable; it *cannot* be present because of the fundamental make-up of the child.

Splitting and projection are intertwined from the start, and in the Kleinian scheme they so characterise the infant's early psychic life that they are emblazoned onto the term used for the earliest developmental period: the 'paranoid schizoid position'. At the earliest possible moment of development, it is claimed, the infant is endangered by its own destructive impulses, which arise from the death drive, and deals with them in the only way it can – by forcing them outwards, projecting them into the external object. This, however, leaves the loving impulses which derive from the life drive at the mercy of a persecutory, harassing external world (hence the 'paranoid' component); in addition, the more mixed up these loving impulses are with the death drive, the more contaminated and spoilt they become. Consequently, in order to save the loving feelings from being poisoned in this way, and also in order to create an ideal object to which the ego can aspire, the derivatives of the life drive are also projected outwards, for 'safe keeping' as it were. Thus, the antagonistic duality of the drives produces in the child's mind a duality of objects, and the breast, which in fact is a single object with rewarding and frustrating aspects, is split in phantasy into the good, nurturing breast and the bad, frustrating one. The child's world is therefore a split one, inside and out, with separate relationships with the persecutory and the loving object, which (from the perspective of early development) have to be kept apart or the former will overwhelm the latter. This split is fundamental; there is no escaping it. However, the *task* of development is to find a way out of this state of extreme splitting so that the ego can learn to deal in a more sophisticated and tolerant way with the actual contradictions of both the internal and external world – can achieve, in a sense, a comprehension of dialectics.

For this movement to occur, Klein claims, the child has to be capable of forging a good internal object on which a more integrated self can be based. Paradoxically perhaps, this can only be achieved if splitting works well, because the good object has to be protected from the potentially devastating assaults of the bad object if it is to survive and grow. As if they were characters in some space age western, Klein imagines the different impulses and objects in the child's mind to be in constant battle with one another: fleeing outwards, taken back in, solidified in their garrisons, assaulted and under siege, seeking reinforcements from elsewhere, gradually consolidating and allowing civilisation to grow. The main aim of the infantile psyche is to introject the ideal object so that it can be the foundation of this civil state; however, this cannot be achieved without the risk that the persecuting object will sneak in and destroy it. So the mind erects its walls, separating the goodies from the baddies in an effort to protect the good internalised object and the psyche as a whole, hoping that splitting will lead to a dispersal of the destructive impulse and therefore of internal persecutory anxieties. Within this 'mind' it is the ego which lies at the centre of the drama. In order to relate to good and bad objects without having the integrity of the latter threatened by the former, the ego splits itself into a 'libidinal' and a 'destructive' part: that is, 'the early ego splits the object and the relation to it in an active way, and this may imply some active splitting of the ego itself'.[2] So, to summarise, what has happened in the early life of the mind is *first* the projection of destructive and good impulses on to an external object, *second*, the splitting of that object into 'bad' and 'good', and *third*, the introjection of those objects to form split ego-object relationships within the psyche.

---

[2] Klein, M. (1946) Notes on Some Schizoid Mechanisms. In M. Klein, *Envy and Gratitude and Other Works* New York: Delta, 1975, p.5

It needs to be remembered that this extraordinary drama is presented as a description of the *normal* formation of the ego's structure in the very early months of life, and that it is also seen as necessary for the ego's survival – without this early splitting, the mind would collapse in on itself. Not only does splitting ensure a separation between good and bad aspects of the psyche and of objects, thus preserving the existence of the good parts from the fury of the bad and enhancing the security of the ego, but it also represents the first strategy for organising the chaotic contents of the mind and hence is fundamental to processes of ordinary thought and discrimination. Without adequate splitting, therefore, there will be cognitive as well as emotional consequences. Psychodynamically, destructive envy would interfere with the split of the initial object into its good and bad aspects (the good object being attacked mercilessly by envious impulses), making the building up of a good object hard to achieve, with synthesis then becoming impossible. Confusion would follow, as good and bad become dangerously muddled up and everything is contaminated by everything else. On the other hand, splitting can be too extreme and come to hamper development or even form the prototype for psychotic breakdowns (for it is recourse to these early defences that is characteristic of schizophrenia).[3] For example, excessive anxiety can bring about too much of a split, leading to fragmentation of the ego which results in it being broken up into unintegratable little bits: 'in order to avoid suffering the ego does its best not to exist, an attempt which gives rise to a specific acute anxiety – that of falling to bits and becoming atomised',[4] this being an example of how defences can cause psychic trouble even as they ward off something worse. In the work of the Kleinian analyst Wilfred Bion, this process is theorised in the rather postmodern-seeming notion of 'bizarre objects', tiny bits of mind which are deliberately disconnected from one another to make them less vulnerable to attack, but have the effect of producing a psychological state which is desperately concrete and dangerous but also mysterious and confusing (nothing relates to anything else) – a prototypically psychotic experience.[5]

---

[3] Klein, M. (1946) Notes on Some Schizoid Mechanisms. In M. Klein, *Envy and Gratitude and Other Works* New York: Delta, 1975, p.5

[4] Segal, H. (1973) *Introduction to the Work of Melanie Klein* London: Hogarth Press, p.31

[5] Bion, W. (1962) *Learning from Experience* London: Maresfield

What Klein seems to be telling us is not only the Freudian story of a fundamental split in consciousness, but a detailed fairy tale of how the activity of splitting is something the mind engages in in order to be able to survive its own passion. Faced with the intensity of infantile emotion – an intensity which does not lessen over a lifetime, even if occasionally it becomes more bearable – and with the difficulty of discerning 'good' from 'bad', love from hate, people lose themselves in fantasies of purity and difference. Here is the ideal, there the devil; here the all-good, there the one embodying evil. Not only, says Klein, are these emblems to be found or invented in the external world, but our inner lives become structured around such splits; we are doubly divided beings, 'vertically' as Freud would have it, between conscious and unconscious (the conscious on the surface, the unconscious the hidden depth), but also 'horizontally', *in* the unconscious itself, between love and hate, life and death. Riven through and through, it seems, integrity may be a hope, but it is not likely ever to be securely attained.

The second account of splitting to have become popular in contemporary thought is probably closer to Freud in that it is concerned with what has to be 'given up' in order to live in a necessarily social world. This account is associated with the work of Jacques Lacan, and in a way it very precisely articulates the paradox that in order to become human, one has to accept not only that not every wish can be achieved, but also that there must be a separation – a 'split' – between what one 'is' and what one can know. In Lacan's version of things, what happens is that the human subject becomes created as a member of society through a process whereby what is essentially a fragmentary, impulse-driven entity becomes organised *along lines given to it from the outside*; hence, it is split by the operations of language and culture, becoming at odds with itself. This process has two key 'moments', which respectively mark the entry into the two Lacanian 'orders' or modes of psychic experience, the Imaginary and the Symbolic. Together, these moments mark a complex process that first thrusts the child into a state of illusory integrity, constituted as the narcissistic identification of the self as a perfect unity, and then fragments this state to produce a language-using social being. It is only when this has occurred that the subject's place in the symbolic world has been found, and the unconscious produced. Additionally, whilst it may seem that only the second 'moment' is truly one of splitting, the first can also be seen this way, for the organisation of the ego as a whole is premised on such an artificial device, that it leaves the individual haunted by another presence – an awareness that all is not as it might seem.

There is a form of splitting right from birth, in Lacan's theory as well as in Klein's, but this is connected to emptiness and absence rather than so clearly to the intense 'fullness' of the drives which is the focus of Kleinian thinking. According to Lacan, there is no absolute unity or primordial oneness from which the neonate proceeds: the primacy of loss is a representation of the notion that the infant is always cut off from the sources of wholeness, always experiences a disjunction between desire and the prospects of fulfilment. This loss is a core element in subjectivity and it defines the child's relations with the world. Most importantly, it is a loss which *cannot be named*: it arises out of the newborn's experience of being separated from the mother who was never 'known' to it in any representational sense, but was positioned as something enveloping, as the neonate's *whole world*. As a consequence, the newborn experiences a drive to recover this loss which can only be appeased through an encounter with an elusive, external object – something wished for but never even conceivable, let alone capable of being found. From the beginning, therefore, the child is constituted in relation to lack and to loss, and that loss has its form in the absence of the object of the child's desire.

At this early point, it makes no sense to think of the infant as a human subject, because there is no sense of difference, no boundary between desire and gratification, no real sense of structure, and because the infant is at the mercy of its drives, inchoate and disorganised as they are. However, even at this stage the child is already *subject to* the desires of others and the restrictions of the immediate social world. At its simplest, for example, the child's own prospects are already structured by the desire that the mother has formed for her or him before birth. The incorporation of this pre-social being into 'subjecthood' properly gets going, however, with the first of the 'moments' mentioned above, the 'mirror phase', and this is deceptively easy to describe.[6] Basically, devastated as it is by its fragmentary nature, torn asunder by the drives, the infant catches a glimpse of its physical integrity in the mirror (the actual mirror or the 'mirror' of the mother's gaze) and identifies with this image, leaping with relief into the fantasy that as a psychological subject it is in fact whole. It is clear here that Lacan's use of the 'mirror' term has nothing to do with the reality of the child's inner drives, but describes a specious representation of integrity, in which the mother presents her own vision *to* her infant but this is taken by the infant to be the 'truth'. The child's perception of her or his 'specular image' thus produces the fiction that she or he is whole and has a clearly ascertainable identity, when what is happening is really that the child is *identifying with* a vision that comes from elsewhere, from outside – an idea which beautifully captures something of the sense of being 'misrecognised' (and of seeing illusions) which is possibly characteristic of contemporary culture. Thus, what is happening here is not that the child actually becomes integrated – as some other analysts such as Winnicott suggest is the function of the mother's mirroring activity – but rather that the ego is used to create an armour or shell supporting the psyche, which is otherwise experienced as in fragments. Lacan emphasises the *exteriority* of this process – that which appears to us as our 'self' is in fact given from the outside as a refuge, an ideal ego, a narcissistically invested image. Hence, although the mirror phase (literally) looks like a form of integration, it is actually a mode of the opposite, of splitting the psyche from its reality.

The second 'moment' of splitting is the moment of entry into language and culture, in which the imaginary wholeness promised by the mirror is shattered by another step of alienation. This is the move to the symbolic order of experience in which the structures of language interfere with the image-making process, revealing that it is already organised by a law indifferent to the emotions and desires of the individual subject. The crucial dynamic here is the entry of the child into language: to speak, to be part of the linguistic order, the subject has to move from the narcissism of the Imaginary to a position from which there is awareness of an outside other, something regulatory which

[6] Lacan, J. (1949) The Mirror Stage as Formative of the Function of the I as Revealed in Psychoanalytic Experience. In J. Lacan, *Ecrits: A Selection* London: Tavistock, 1977

takes the form of a law. The 'Symbolic order' thus positions the individual as a separate, speaking entity, with her or his subjectivity organised along specifiable routes. To speak meaningfully, that is, one has to accept the existence of a language which one has not invented oneself, but which exists externally and exerts constraints. Once again, this positioning arises from outside the subject, confirming its self-alienation: 'I identify myself in language, but only by losing myself in it like an object'.[7] Thus, the positioning of the subject with respect to language requires an encounter with otherness in a way that fractures the omnipotence of the mirrored 'I' in the Imaginary. If the Imaginary celebrates the fictitious identity of subject and ego, it is the tearing of this identity that moves the subject into the Symbolic order, and at the same time constructs the unconscious: what is 'left out' becomes repressed.

In the terms used earlier, Lacan emphasises the 'vertically' split nature of the human subject, the sense in which it is constructed through a process of division, and gains its essential characteristics from this division. The subject can never be present to itself because the only formulation that can be made is through language, in which the subject appears as an alienated 'I', constructed in the discourses that surround it. More fully, the insertion of the human subject into language depends on an experience of otherness, of absence and of lack: it is only by the perception of a boundary between self and other, and hence of the impossibility of total fulfilment, that the child can formulate a communicable notion of the self; hence, in all its experiences in language, the subject is constantly reiterating its division. The thrust of development is therefore not towards greater integration (as in Klein's work), but towards greater division, as the entry into the order of culture constructs the unconscious and sexuality in the awareness of a fundamental absence of gratification. Moreover, whereas Klein proposes that there is an active ego present at birth which splits defensively in order to protect itself against anxiety, Lacan stresses the ways in which we can only operate through the division and alienation language institutes; that is, we are *constituted as split*

---

[7] Lacan, J. (1953) The Function and Field of Speech and Language in Psychoanalysis. In J. Lacan, *Ecrits: A Selection* London: Tavistock, 1977, p.86

rather than splitting.[8] So to Lacan's slogan, 'There is no sexual relation': this is, as Jacqueline Rose explains[9], because the unconscious divides subjects from one another (so no full relationship of any kind is possible) even as it infuses them with the desire for unification.

[8] Benjamin, J. (1998) *Shadow of the Other: Intersubjectivity and Gender in Psychoanalysis* New York: Routledge, p.88

[9] Rose, J. (1982) Introduction – II. In J. Mitchell and J. Rose (eds) *Feminine Sexuality* London: Macmillan

6 Phantasy

PSYCHOANALYSIS is best thought of as the discipline devoted to the study of unconscious life; to a considerable degree, this means the study of unconscious mental contents or phantasies. The notion of 'phantasy' here is, as with many psychoanalytic terms, not straightforward; moreover, it is developed differently – and more comprehensively – in Kleinian theory than in Freudian. Still, there is nothing so very surprising in the concept itself: Laplanche and Pontalis give the following definition, which makes it clear that sometimes phantasies are simply strategies for wishing away reality, whereas at other times they are the stuff of unconscious life.

Imaginary scene in which the subject is a protagonist, representing the fulfilment of a wish (in the last analysis, an unconscious wish) in a manner that is distorted to a greater or lesser extent by defensive processes. Phantasy has a number of different modes: conscious phantasies or day-dreams, unconscious phantasies like those uncovered by analysis as the structures underlying a manifest content, and primal phantasies.[1]

The second and third of these 'modes' of phantasy have been the main focus of post-Freudian attention, so much so that in English the first mode ('conscious phantasies or day-dreams') is usually spelt *fantasy*, precisely to distinguish it as a form of conscious rather than unconscious psychological activity. So a fantasy is a conscious wish, something which is known to be at odds with actual reality; though it is not necessarily impossible (it may be a plausible imaginary scene of future success, for example), it is not really there, it is illusory.

So far so good; fantasy and reality are different. However, this commonsensical idea turns out to be deeply problematic when one allows

---

[1] Laplanche, J. and Pontalis, J.-B. (1973) *The Language of Psychoanalysis* London: Hogarth Press, p.314

for the existence of the unconscious as a kind of continuous causal commentary on psychic activity. If, as Freud implies, the unconscious is constantly active, that is, *dynamic*, with ideas and wishes bubbling up, held repressed by defensive manoeuvres but also demanding compromises, creating distortions and lying at the root of motivated activity – if, that is, the unconscious pervades all thinking – then there can be no unbiased realistic perception, no simple distinction between what we are 'imagining' and what we know to be real. Restlessly pursuing expression, unconscious phantasies keep welling up, to such a degree that wherever one looks in a person's life – their dreams, their plans, their pictures, their judgements – one finds evidence at least of some unconscious component. Laplanche and Pontalis argue, therefore, that in psychoanalysis the distinction between reality and fantasy/phantasy will always break down.

As the investigation progresses, even aspects of behaviour that are far removed from imaginative activity, and which appear at first glance to be governed solely by the demands of reality, emerge as emanations, as 'derivatives' of unconscious phantasy. In the light of this evidence, it is the subject's life as a whole which is seen to be shaped and ordered by what might be called, in order to stress this structuring action, 'a phantasmatic'.[2]

It is this realisation, that phantasy is simply the name given to the endless materialisations of unconscious life, which governs the Kleinian account.

For Freud, phantasies were always specifically motivated as responses to frustration – substitutes for what could not be achieved in the real world, just as dreams are substitute fulfilments of untenable wishes. For Klein, however, everything that happens, psychologically speaking, arises from a bed of phantasy; the production of unconscious ideas is simply *what the mind does*, beginning at the start of life as mental representations of the biological life and death drives. That is, there is no need to explain the existence of phantasies by postulating frustration, as, for example, in the situation where the child 'imagines' the presence of a mother who has in fact gone away, or a breast which has been withdrawn. Rather, the mind is always active, constantly generating unconscious ideas, and it is through the lens produced by these

[2] Ibid. p.317

ideas that 'reality' is perceived. 'Phantasy is not merely an escape from reality, but a constant and unavoidable accompaniment of real experiences, constantly interacting with them.'[3] Indeed, Kleinians view phantasy as the basic stuff of psychological functioning, without which there would be no mental processes at all.

The internal phantasy world has absolute primacy in this model, and all that we do, think and feel depends upon it. Additionally, because this inner world exists as 'really' and as primordially as the external one, the latter can never be experienced in a pure form. Rather, the outside world is always perceived and related to through a screen of the child's internal drives and phantasies, which may alter its impact dramatically. Correspondingly, the inner phantasies are themselves alterable, both because of the gradual maturing of the infant's bodily experience so that expulsion and ingestion need not be the only models for psychological activity (though, as projection and introjection, they remain amongst the most powerful), and also because of the impact of social or interpersonal experiences on the content of mental phantasies. For example, the presence of a genuinely containing environment – that is, a mother who can manage her infant's distress and hatred – allows the violence and threat of the earliest destructive phantasies to be ameliorated, and hence moves the infant towards a more integrated state of mind. What Kleinians term the 'paranoid schizoid position' is characterised by the earlier form of phantasy, in which destructiveness and love have to be held apart and projected outwards; with the later 'depressive position' comes this more integrated state of mind.

Kleinians emphasise that these are not just developmental stages but also psychic attitudes; that is, throughout life our phantasies fluctuate between more fissiparous and more integrative possibilities. Moreover, this is a fluctuation between more concrete and more symbolic (hence, 'mature') modes of thought, showing again how phantasy underpins all forms of mental activity. Wilfred Bion expresses this well with his distinction between 'β' elements and 'α' elements, the former being the undigested, raw material of experience, concrete blocks which must be worked on and shaped by α-function if they are

---

[3] Segal, H. (1973) *Introduction to the Work of Melanie Klein* London: Hogarth Press, p.14

to be integrated into the thinking and creative life of the person. Alpha-function itself is the process of thought, that which transforms experience from one mode to another, making it 'digestible'.

Alpha-function operates on the sense impressions, whatever they are, and the emotions, of which the patient is aware. In so far as α-function is successful, α-elements are produced and these elements are suited to storage and the requirements of dream thoughts . . . In contrast with the α-elements, β-elements are not felt to be phenomena, but things in themselves.[4]

Mental life is constituted, the claim goes, by these unconscious thought processes, modified through experience (Bion's book on the subject is called *Learning from Experience*) but always there in one form or another, whether paranoid, psychotic or depressed, such being the main choices Kleinians allow.

Finally, this insistence on the centrality of phantasy to the psycho-analytic endeavour has a significant impact on therapeutic practice and theory. If phantasy is always present rather than being a substitute for an accurate representation of reality, then the work of analysis cannot be understood as redressing distortions of feeling or thinking, but rather has to be seen as a process of working with and through the continuous production of unconscious ideas, some of which may be more disturbing and extreme than others, but all of which will be 'phantastic'. This produces a focus in Kleinian therapy on the here-and-now interchange between patient and analyst, and recasts the idea of transference as something which *always occurs*, rather than being a product of essentially remediable distorted or mistaken perceptions. For example, in the context of child analysis,

The practice of Kleinian psychoanalysis has become an understanding of the transference as an expression of unconscious phantasy, active right here and now in the moment of the analysis.[5]

In this formulation, it ceases to be possible to distinguish realistic aspects of the therapist-patient interaction from imaginary ones, for all reality is read through the lens of phantasy, and is half constructed

---

[4] Bion, W. (1962) *Learning from Experience* London: Maresfield, p.6
[5] Hinshelwood, R. (1991) *A Dictionary of Kleinian Thought* London: Free Association Books, p.465

as it is perceived. The analytic relationship becomes a field of phantasy; any discrimination between internal and external worlds is made fragile and unconvincing. The Freudian conceptualisation of the transference as a kind of irrational error, a misreading of the present in terms of the past, gives way to a more fluid and fertile understanding in which current emotions and self-representations, formed initially by past experiences but nevertheless alive and growing in the present, take precedence.

7 Identification

THAT psychoanalysis is concerned with the 'inner world' is hardly news, but one important and largely unresolved question this raises is how do things – ideas, representations of self and others, unconscious desires – get 'into' it. Many psychoanalytic theories assume that at least some of these things start inside: these are the drives and, in some accounts, basic pre-given ideas such as primitive representations of objects or of the self. However, all psychoanalysts from Freud onwards have postulated the existence of mechanisms whereby external experiences are *taken* in; that is, it is assumed that shape and content is given to the mind by events and people outside it, which are somehow made its own. The mind is in constant dialogue with the world, putting into it some of its own contents (through projection, for example) and finding ways of producing internal representations of what it finds there. Without such engagement, it would consist only of what was produced from within; it would be a 'closed system', generating meanings on the basis perhaps of drives or in response to external stimuli, but unable to absorb features of the outside world into itself.

There is nothing in itself surprising or novel in this claim; after all, perception, learning and memory are obvious everyday instances of ways in which each of us absorbs information 'from outside' and incorporates it into our existing internal stock of knowledge. But what psychoanalysis claims actually happens is not only that external stimuli are processed by the perceptual system, but more radically that they are somehow 'internalised', taken in to become part of the mind, infecting its structure and – most importantly – its unconscious contents. That is, psychoanalysis models an 'open system' in which external experiences – encounters with 'objects', relationships, ideas – can become part of the person in a deep way. At its most sophisticated, what this produces is a theory in which 'self' and 'other' are always entwined, so that there is no way of considering any mind in isolation from any other. Hinshelwood, writing out of the Kleinian tradition in which there is an emphasis on processes of projection and introjection operating from birth, phrases this about as strongly as could ever be:

> The internal objects are phantasies, but at first phantasies are omnipotent, so through these primitive phantasies involved in identification the object *is* the self . . . Phantasy 'is' reality, and phantasy constructs the reality of the internal world on the basis of these primitive forms of introjective and projective identification.[1]

That is, because the infant is always engaged in a process of 'putting out and taking in', of projecting feelings into the external 'object' and then seeking to absorb properties of these objects, the emerging psyche is filled with representations, however crude, of the object, and it is around these object representations that it becomes structured. Hence, there is no firm division between inside and out, but rather a fluid interchange in which each penetrates the other.

Moore and Fine define 'internalisation' as 'a process by which aspects of the outer world and interactions with it are taken into the organism and represented in its internal structure', with the three principal routes to this being the slightly differing notions of 'incorporation, introjection and identification'.[2] Identification itself is seen by them as the most organised of these principles of internalisation, based on the clearest differentiation between subject and object, although they also acknowledge overlap and the tendency amongst many analysts to adopt a general view of identificatory processes. Thus, they note that identification 'is often used in a generic sense to refer to all the mental processes by which an individual becomes like another in one or several aspects'.[3] This is reasonably distinct from *incorporation*, which often implies a kind of internal destruction of the object (swallowing something up) and also (though less clearly) from *introjection*, which can refer to emotions as well as aspects of the

---

[1] Hinshelwood, R. (1991) *A Dictionary of Kleinian Thought* London: Free Association Books, p.320
[2] Moore, B. and Fine, B. (1990) *Psychoanalytic Terms and Concepts* New Haven: Yale University Press, p.102
[3] Ibid. p.103

other and which also implies a kind of bodily symbolisation of the object, albeit this time not as destroyed. Laplanche and Pontalis also choose to differentiate identification from internalisation on the grounds of their *relational structure*: 'From a purely conceptual point of view we may say that he identifies with *objects* – i.e. with a person ("the assimilation of one ego to another one"), with a characteristic of a person, or with a part-object – whereas he internalises intersubjective *relations*'[4]. However, this seems rather forced, given the inextricability of 'objects' from the relations that surround them, and it is perhaps best to acknowledge a variety of overlaps of meaning and yet be satisfied with a general notion of identification as the process whereby an individual takes in attributes of the people with whom she or he is in contact, and is transformed as a consequence.

Thought of that way, identification is a constructive process, in that the internalised attributes are not destroyed but are employed in the service of some kind of development (hence, it remains distinct from incorporation in the psychoanalytic sense), and it is likely that it is one of the most powerful methods whereby the self changes. Freud for one seemed to recognise this, even though his theory implies that the first 'thoughts' are representations of the drives, coming from within rather than without. In his later work in particular, Freud argued that the ego is constructed on the basis of identifications, being 'a precipitate of abandoned object cathexes and that it contains the history of these object choices'.[5] As his work progressed, indeed, so identification became seen as more central. This is particularly the case in relation to the Oedipus complex, the outcome of which is theorised as a set of powerful identifications (for the boy, especially with the father) laying the foundations of all later personality development. That is, as the boy, threatened with the castrating power of the father, represses his desire for the mother, so what emerges for him is a saving identification with the father which creates gender security as well as the promise of later recovery. For the girl too, even though the processes described by Freud are more confused and less potent, there is an identification with

---

[4] Laplanche, J. and Pontalis, J.-B. (1973) *The Language of Psychoanalysis* London: Hogarth Press, p.208

[5] Freud, S. (1923) The Ego and the Id. In S. Freud, *On Metapsychology* Harmondsworth: Penguin, 1984, p.368

the mother's position in relation to the father that leads to the gendered channelling of desire. In addition, the construction of the superego as a response to castration anxiety is one big identificatory process: what is taken in here is the phantasy of the paternal prohibition, with all its associated aggression.

For post-Freudians, identification has become ever more central. Thus, object relations theorists tend to assume that the drives (if they exist at all) are always directed towards objects, and hence that mental contents are based on an internalising procedure. In this work, the identifications made in early life between mother and infant have particularly profound causal consequences for later development. One especially influential version of this claim, because of its relationship to wider social ideas about women's development, comes from certain strands of feminist object relations theory which make the differential pattern of identifications between mothers and daughters and mothers and sons crucial for the construction of gender identities. Here is a summary statement which captures the main point.

In mothering a baby girl a woman is bringing her daughter up to be like her, to be a girl and then a woman. In mothering her son she is bringing him up to be other, to be a boy and then a man.[6]

These writers postulate several aspects of the mother-daughter relationship that shape a girl's psychology, employing a two-way notion of identification, from mother to daughter and back again, in a move creating out of psychoanalysis a more thoroughly 'interpersonal' theory. First, the *mother* identifies with her daughter and projects on to her the same feelings that she has about herself; she acts towards her daughter in the way that she unconsciously relates to her own repressed 'little girl' aspect, including all the baggage of self-denigration and lack of confidence produced in women by patriarchy. Secondly, the ambivalence created by this pattern of identification leads to a peculiarly staccato quality and possible inconsistency in the mother's handling of her child, creating conditions of oscillating frustration and gratification that make a child feel overpowered and rejected. The consequence for the daughter is that she recognises in herself the 'little girl' rejected by

⁶ Eichenbaum, L. and Orbach, S. (1982) *Outside In . . . Inside Out* Harmondsworth: Penguin, p.30

the mother, identifies with it but also splits it off, hiding it through repression and relating to the world through a series of false personal boundaries. Most importantly, through identification with the mother coupled with the experiences of frustration by her, the daughter learns to lose her expectations of being nurtured and instead to become extremely sensitive to the needs of others: 'she learns to give what others need; she starts to give to others out of the well of her own unmet needs'.[7]

A more subtle rendering of gender identifications has been given more recently by the American feminist psychoanalyst, Jessica Benjamin. Holding onto the distinction between identification and incorporation, the latter being a kind of cannibalistic taking in of the other until it becomes part of the self, no longer psychically distinct, Benjamin argues that what is precious about identification is that it allows the other to *survive* as a living and appreciated aspect of the self. Identification is consequently built out of an already-existing awareness of the other's existence *as a subject*; that is, it is a loving 'intersubjective' relationship in which aspects of otherness are accepted and used by the self, without destroying the other in the process. In Benjamin's words:

Identificatory love is a specific formation, it is the love that wants to be recognised by the other as like. Identification is not merely a matter of incorporating the other as ideal, but of loving and having a relationship with the person who embodies the ideal.[8]

Identification can thus be seen as a form of *relationship*, not just a way in which one person acts upon another; developmentally, for example, it can be a way in which a boy aspires to be linked to his father rather than to be rivalrous with him. Indeed, in the context of gender development Benjamin claims that boys and girls both identify with the loving father, just as they do with the powerful and loving mother, making multiple identifications along the way. The effect of these multiple identifications is to produce in the child a greater range of possible gender positions, particularly enhancing 'complementarity'

[7] Ibid. p.38
[8] Benjamin, J. (1998) *Shadow of the Other: Intersubjectivity and Gender in Psychoanalysis* New York: Routledge, p.61

rather than the kind of exclusivity which results in the triumph of one gender position over another.

On the basis of such complex patterns of identification in which the child incorporates aspects of all her or his loved objects into the self, it is possible to recast development as a process of making increasingly fine internal differentiations which does not necessarily (depending on the quality of actual object relationships) take place at the expense of the valuing of difference. That is, the classic view of identification, particularly in the Oedipus complex, is that it involves taking in one thing and repudiating another. Benjamin, however, outlines a more mature, post-Oedipal complementarity which brings back together the various 'elements of identification, so that they become less threatening, less diametrically opposite, no longer cancelling out one's identity'.[9] Multiple identifications forge the basis for identities (including gender identities) which themselves are multiple and fluid, less defensive and hence less caricatured and stereotyped. *Connectedness* is emphasised here, recognising difference but not discounting the other because of it.

This optimistic rendering of identification with others as a way of taking in multiple possibilities for development is one important strand in contemporary work. However, a critical alternative is derived from the work of Lacan, who saw identification as an 'imaginary' process of taking on an image and 'appropriating' it as if it represents the self. That is, identification is primarily a way of losing oneself in the other; more precisely, the fact that identification is at the root of the formation of the ego reveals that the ego is itself 'specious', a false acceptance of an image as real. In his commentary on Freud's famous dream of 'Irma's injection', Lacan makes this point particularly strongly.

[The] ego is the sum of the identifications of the subject, with all that that implies as to its radical contingency. If you allow me to give an image of it, the ego is like the superimposition of various coats borrowed from what I will call the bric-à-brac of its props department.[10]

[9] Benjamin, J. (1998) *Shadow of the Other: Intersubjectivity and Gender in Psychoanalysis* New York: Routledge, pp.69–70

[10] Lacan, J. (1954-5) *The Seminars of Jacques Lacan, Book II: The Ego in Freud's Theory and in the Technique of Psychoanalysis* Cambridge: Cambridge University Press; p.155. The 'Irma' dream is to be found in Freud, S. (1900) *The Interpretation of Dreams* Harmondsworth: Penguin, 1976

The ego is here described as 'the sum of the identifications of the subject'. Identification, psychoanalysis attests, is that process whereby the ego takes the object and makes it *subject*, incorporating each object as part of itself. According to Lacan, this is indeed a formative process, but its effect is specifically to create a kind of radical misperception, in which the ego is taken to be the 'truth' of the person when it is actually just 'bric-à-brac', made up of bits and pieces latched onto from outside. Hence there is a sense in which identification *falsifies*, with the subject 'using' the object to sustain a fantasy of integrity of the self. This is why Lacan was opposed to the idea that psychoanalytic psychotherapy should aim at enabling the patient to identify with the analyst; rather, he suggested, analysis should aim to show the patient how identifications are all impossibly fantastic. No-one can become the model for another; instead, suggests Lacan, the 'real' of the subject lies outside what can be organised and known. Identification, therefore, may well be a major mechanism through which what is outside comes to be registered within, but this also makes it a mode of alienation, whereby the human subject is made a stranger to itself.

8 Oedipus Complex

IF there is one concept that has captured the excesses of psychoanalysis in the minds of many people – the 'general public' – it is that of the Oedipus complex. As in the joke, 'Oedipus, schmoedipus, he's just a boy who loves his mother', the idea that every boy wishes to sleep with his mother and is warned off this only by the overpowering anxiety of being castrated by his father, figures somewhere near (or over) the borders of the believable. The theory of the Oedipus complex has been criticised as too extreme, ethnocentric, patriarchal and misogynist. It has even been attacked as a wilful misreading of the Oedipus myth itself, in which the initial hatred comes from the father Laius, afraid his baby son will supplant him – that is, the fear is the father's, not the son's. It is seen as the paradigm of a psychoanalytic tendency to take a vaguely, mythologically cast theory, impossible to test or even to specify clearly, declare it to be universal and make belief in it the touchstone of orthodoxy, so that it becomes imposed like a grid on all experience. The Oedipus complex is thus a 'belief' rather than an objective 'discovery', perhaps even a wish in the mind of Freud, rather than a fact.

All this, and more, is true, yet the Oedipus complex retains both cultural and psychoanalytic resonance well in excess of what might be expected given its tenuous hold on reality. To understand why this is so, it is necessary to explore the way in which the Oedipus complex has come to be seen not so much as an account of the actual experiences of every child at the hands of her or his parents, but rather as a meditation on the way in which unconscious desire is limited, organised and structured through the activities of the social world. That is, with all its wildness, the theory of the Oedipus complex has proved to be a seminal myth for symbolising how the unconscious is socialised. Along with Freud's claim that the ego is built up on the basis of the internalisation of lost objects, the Oedipus complex is the prime site for observation of the operation of internalisation and identification – for the process of 'taking in' that which is outside (here, the regulations on sexuality imposed by the father or, more generally, by the social order) and making it central to the psyche. After Oedipus, there is no clear distinction between inside and out, for each infuses the other with what it wants.

The starting point for understanding the Oedipus complex is the idea, central to Freud's thought, that humans are governed by biological drives, the most significant of which is the sexual drive. This drive operates from birth – hence the notion of 'infantile sexuality' – in an unrelenting way, building tension out of a succession of gradually maturing body parts (the oral, anal and phallic 'sources' of the drive) and seeking satisfaction through increasingly diverse pathways (the drive's 'objects'). Sexuality does not 'begin' anywhere, it rather becomes organised into different structures, usually seen by Freud as increasingly sophisticated and normative, but always showing the residues of their earlier, more 'polymorphously perverse' forms. At the start of life, most analysts agree, the drives are relatively 'primitive' and undifferentiated, finding satisfaction in 'part objects' (mainly the breast). The desire of the child gradually matures in its transition from oral, to anal to phallic bodily parts, but also in consequence of the child's increasing cognitive capacity to understand that 'whole objects' exist, that is, that the breast is not the mother, but part of her, and – ominously – that outside her stands a father. In Melanie Klein's work, it should be noted, this realisation is given the full weight of a move from a more 'split' emotional state to a more integrated one, expressed as a transition from the 'paranoid schizoid position' to the 'depressive position' allowing awareness of the complexity of other people and the ambivalence of the child's own feelings towards them.

So, from birth the child has experienced sexual wishes, directed towards the objects which satisfy them, notably the mother's breast. At a certain point of development, dated by Freud as when the child is between three to five years of age, the sexual drive becomes organised around the penis or clitoris (the phallic stage) and its object becomes the 'whole' mother. It is at this point that a prohibition occurs, which for the boy is catastrophic and for the girl is at least formative (and, in truth, obscure): for what is effectively the first time the social world, represented by the father, says 'no: this far and no further you may go; this wish cannot be enacted'. Thus, the child's 'natural' incestuous desire, operating without consideration of the conventions that determine what is or is not an acceptable sexual object, is opposed by a 'non-natural' incest taboo, which structures this desire into a socialised form. 'So long as the community assumes no other form than the family,' writes Freud, showing some awareness of possible cultural specificity, 'the conflict is bound to express itself in the Oedipus complex.'[1]

Under the sway of the Oedipus complex, the male child's desire for the mother is contradicted by paternal authority backed up by the father's real and imagined power to harm him, which Freud conceptualises as appearing in the boy's mind as the threat of castration. The child's consequent terror within the 'castration complex' results in him renouncing (repressing) his passion for the mother and identifying with the father. Included in this identification is not just the promise of deferred gratification, that later on he can take the place of the father, but also a deeply internalised aggressivity, derived both from the boy's hostility towards the father and his phantasy that the father is murderously hostile towards him. What happens is that this threat not only forces the repression of sexual desire, but institutes a new 'structure' within the mind, the superego or 'Over-I' (Über-Ich), the source of an unconscious but continuing scrutiny of a person's wishes, ensuring not only that there is no forbidden *activity*, but even that illicit *ideas* are kept out of awareness. Freud says about this, 'Civilization . . . obtains mastery over the individual's dangerous desire for aggression by disarming it and by setting up an agency within him to watch over it, like a garrison in a conquered city.'[2] This is, in essence, the model for all the individual's encounters with society: desire opposed by authority, authority internalised and made one's own.

The structure of the developmental account here, at least for the boy, is reasonably clear: the child's sexual desire, directed towards the

[1] Freud, S. (1930) Civilization and its Discontents. In S. Freud, *Civilisation, Society and Religion* Harmondsworth: Penguin, 1985, p.325

[2] Ibid., p.316

mother, is blocked by the prohibitive force of the father and becomes repressed. Alongside this arises an identification with the father which holds out the promise of later on becoming like him both in power and in sexual authority; this whole situation is policed through the internalisation of aggression and with it the father's castrating power. The father here, patently, embodies the constraining force of a society which is in essence opposed to the expression of the child's omnipotent, unbridled desires: for society to function, laws and regulations have to be imposed. Hence the response to the widespread question: what about children who grow up in fatherless homes? To a considerable extent, the presence or absence of the actual father is irrelevant to the existence of the Oedipus complex, although it does make a difference to its intensity. This is because the Oedipal father is not just (or even) the child's real father, who may be threatening or gentle, nurturing or absent; rather, he is the *symbol* of patriarchal authority, through which social norms are enforced. The Oedipal father is a representation of what society allows in terms of the expression of desire and through this also of sexual difference, of what is male and female: one pattern of identifications is promoted in the boy, another in the girl. This is why so many writers emphasise the function of the Oedipus complex as a *law*: it regulates, differentiating between the many biologically and psychologically possible things a person may wish and do. Juliet Mitchell, for example, states that it 'governs the position of each person in the triangle father, mother and child; in the way it does this, it embodies the law that founds the human order itself'.[3] For Laplanche and Pontalis, the Oedipus complex describes the triangular configuration 'constituted by the child, the child's natural object, and the bearer of the law'.[4] The real father slips away in this; what emerges instead is a description of the impossibility of interpersonal relationships that are not already structured by something outside them, this being the 'law' by which society operates. More fully and intriguingly, given the roots of psychoanalysis in drive theory, what begins as a biological urge (sexual desire) becomes channelled through the internalisation of an 'object relationship' (the

---

[3] Mitchell, J. (1982) Introduction – I. In J. Mitchell and J. Rose (eds) *Feminine Sexuality* London: Macmillan, p.14

[4] Laplanche, J. and Pontalis, J.-B. (1973) *The Language of Psychoanalysis* London: Hogarth Press, p.286

imagined, mostly threatening relationship with the father), to produce a new structure for the mind. This has been taken up, in post-Freudian work, as the template for a more intersubjective view of psychological development, which understands the relationships made by a child to be the principal organising force in her or his mental life.

In what has been described above, the emphasis has been on the classical Oedipus complex associated with the male child's development. There are some important qualifiers here, however. The first refers to the difference between the 'positive' and 'negative' forms of the Oedipus complex, with the former being along the lines just described, and the latter being characterised by love for the parent of the *same* sex, and jealous hatred for the parent of the opposite sex. The complete arrangement of the Oedipus complex involves a mix of both positive and negative complexes, laying down a rich tapestry of possibilities for homosexual as well as heterosexual love. 'The description of the complex in its complete form allows Freud to elucidate ambivalence towards the father (in the case of the little boy) in terms of the play of heterosexual and homosexual components, instead of making it simply the result of a situation of rivalry.'[5] This complexity means that in any individual case it is (or should be – psychoanalysts have not always followed their own theory consistently) extremely hard to explain development straightforwardly in Oedipal terms: for every desire there is a counter-desire, every identification holds in train its opposite.

The second 'caveat' is the story of female development, which in Freud's hands is rather a sorry tale, but which in later psychoanalysis has been a source of immensely creative friction. According to Freud, the girl's Oedipus complex is not a simple parallel to, or inversion of, that of the boy (hence his rejection of Jung's term 'Electra complex'), a position followed by most later psychoanalysts, perhaps especially Lacan, who emphasises that in every case, male or female, what the child has to come to terms with is the structuring power of the *father's* authority and the relinquishment of a desire for the first object of infantile love, the mother. However, whereas many later analysts

[5] Laplanche, J. and Pontalis, J.-B. (1973) *The Language of Psychoanalysis* London: Hogarth Press, p.284

assert that it is the boy who has more trouble reaching his gendered identity, because he must 'dis-identify' with the powerful object he knows (the mother) and instead base his masculinity on a father who is mysterious, threatening and often absent, Freud assumes that it is the girl child who must deal with the more difficult developmental process. This is because she must cope with two emotional moves not required of the boy and both involving painful loss: first, giving up her phallic, male focus on her own 'penis', the clitoris, and, secondly, transferring her desire from the mother to the father. In effect, this means that whereas the boy child uses his repression-and-identification strategy as a way of *avoiding* castration, the girl has to learn how to respond to the realisation that she is *already* 'castrated', a fairly devastating blow, one would imagine. In more detail, the story goes as follows. Until the phallic phase, male and female development run in parallel, as children of both sexes are attached to the mother and both boys and girls experience similar oral and anal impulses. Most significantly, both are bisexual: that is, both boys and girls contain masculine *and* feminine elements, albeit in differing proportions due to biological variations (though differing within members of the same sex as well as between the sexes). But the phallic stage creates new problems. The centre of sexual excitement for the boy shifts from the anus to the penis, his desire becoming that of penetration and possession of the mother. For the girl, the leading erotic zone is the clitoris. However, according to Freud, it cannot remain so: 'With the change to femininity the clitoris should wholly or in part hand over its sensitivity, and at the same time its importance, to the vagina'.[6] The little girl, dependent on her clitoris for sexual stimulation becomes aware of how small it is in comparison to the boy's penis and assumes that because of this it must also be *inferior* as an organ, an assumption which does not actually seem necessary, but which Freud and many other analysts, male and female, have thought must be so. This leads the girl to experience a mixture of impassioned and negative emotions: a general sense of her own inferiority in the world linked with the relative ineffectiveness of her genitals in providing satisfaction for

---

[6] Freud, S. (1933) *New Introductory Lectures on Psychoanalysis* Harmondsworth: Penguin, 1973, pp.151–2

the sexual drive, a hateful rage at the mother for having created her like that, in her own image, and a passionate envy of the real thing, the penis possessed by father and brother alike. The girl thus shifts from mother-love to father-love because everything worthwhile resides in the latter. In line with the reversal of the boy's trajectory mentioned above, the girl's castration complex – that is, her recognition of herself as already castrated – pushes her into the Oedipus situation, in which her desire is to displace the mother in order to get for herself a share in the father's power. This is why, according to Freud, young girls feel strong unconscious hostility towards their mothers; it is also the source of the shift of sexual object from mother to father necessary for normative, heterosexual femininity. Thus, *failures* of this Oedipal realignment of sexual desire can lead to lesbianism and/or neurosis. Finally, the girl's desire for the penis must itself be renounced and replaced by the desire for a baby, 'in accordance with an ancient symbolic equivalence'; with masculine fervour, Freud suggests that the mother's happiness 'is great if later on this wish for a baby finds fulfilment in reality and quite especially so if the baby is a little boy who brings the longed-for penis with him'.[7] The rather startling implication here is that boys tend to be valued more than girls not for economic or ideological reasons, but because boy children supply what women really want, a desire which may be repressed but which is never lost, a penis the same as a man's.

It hardly needs saying that this account of female development has created enduring scandal throughout the history of psychoanalysis. Freud himself recognised the provisional nature of his understanding of femininity, and early on some major psychoanalysts, mainly women, were willing to risk this as an arena for disagreement with him. The characteristic feature of the opposition was to deny Freud's idea that femininity develops through a growing awareness of lack and absence in comparison with men, an account which places at the centre of the female mind a desire to be male. Their argument, in general, was that the fact that the first love-object of both sexes is the mother does not mean that girls are 'little men' as Freud would have it;

---

[7] Freud, S. (1933) *New Introductory Lectures on Psychoanalysis* Harmondsworth: Penguin, 1973, p.162

nor are girls necessarily different from boys in their ideas about loss and threats to their personality. *All* children fear 'castration' in the sense of being impressed above all with their lack of power in the world – that is, they have dependency needs and fear abandonment. In addition, some analysts such as Melanie Klein and Karen Horney emphasised, against Freud, the power of the *mother* in the child's mind: 'in my experience', wrote Klein, 'the woman's penis envy can be traced back to envy of the mother's breast'.[8] Horney went furthest in all this by suggesting that Freud's account of femininity is fixed at the level of the four-year-old boy who cannot bear to envision the reality of a girl's separate sexuality, but must defend himself by disparagement of her capabilities. This fixation, she held, prevented Freud from recognising the specificity of female development and hence developing an adequate psychology of women.[9]

In the post-Freudian world, too, there has been violent dispute. Lacan, for example, consistently reasserted Freud's position on femininity, whilst also reading the Oedipus complex as entwined with the structures of language and society. He therefore offered an account of sexual development which could be taken either as deliberately culturally specific – an exposition of patriarchy – or as deterministic, implying that all cultures are based on the exclusion of women. This arises out of Lacan's idea that the Oedipus complex is a portal into a different order of experience, the Symbolic order of language and culture which, as the 'Law of the Father', structures all interactions, even the early extraordinarily intimate ones between mother and infant. This Law *is* the way the social world is organised, compelling the taking up of gendered positions and making anatomical differences between male and female the principal axis along which development occurs. All encounters between people are organised according to this Law; for example, in order to communicate linguistically at all with one another, it is necessary to bow to the structures of meaning embedded in specific languages. For the same reason that Freud saw the Oedipal father as defining reality for the child – that is, because the

---

[8] Klein, M. (1957) Envy and Gratitude. In M. Klein, *Envy and Gratitude and Other Works* New York: Delta, 1975, p.199

[9] Horney, K. (1926) Flight from Womanhood *International Journal of Psychoanalysis 7*, 324–339

father places a limit on narcissistic fantasy – Lacan claims that these structures derive from the 'No' of the father: they depend on recognising that complete possession of the other, complete wholeness, is impossible and that something exists outside the mother-infant bond. Whatever happens, Lacanians assert, the father embodies power, and there is no way around that. On the other hand, some post-Lacanian feminists have asserted that there is a specific form of female power neglected by psychoanalysis, a power embodied particularly in the mother – a position which partially aligns them with Klein's theory. More straightforwardly, object relations theorists have tended to argue that the Oedipus complex is over-valued in psychoanalysis, and that more attention needs to be paid to pre-Oedipal development. When this imbalance is redressed, a theory is produced which emphasises identification rather than sexual desire, and the problematic issue becomes that of explaining how a boy finds his gendered identification with his father from a position of having been absorbed in his mother. That is, from this perspective one could suggest that the little boy is a little woman, in place of Freud's assertion that the 'little girl is a little man'.

There is an other set of concerns about the Oedipus complex which has been exercising many contemporary psychoanalysts and which cuts to the heart of much psychoanalytic developmental thinking. The way in which the story is formulated suggests that in the pre-Oedipal period there is only a vague appreciation of the demands of reality. Instead, the child is enveloped in a fantasy of a 'narcissistic' link to the mother in which every wish can be met, in which what is desired can always come to be. In this version of things, the great achievement of the Oedipal phase is to lift the child out of this narcissistic state and into one in which the demands and regulations of reality can be appreciated – when, for example, the specifics of sex and gender, of generational difference and of language, can be understood, and their demands accepted. Without the Oedipal regulation of desire, it is held, there will be no acknowledgement of reality, and therefore there will be narcissistic disorders of the 'psychotic' type; acceptance of sexual repression, identification with the same-sex parent, love only for the heterosexual other, these are the necessary price to be paid for living in the real world.

There have always been critiques of this set of assumptions, ranging from Wilhelm Reich's accusation that the 'authoritarian family' produces fascism, through to the infamous assault on psychoanalysis in Deleuze and Guattari's book, *Anti-Oedipus*.[10] Others have attempted to reorient psychoanalytic thinking to take account properly of the *parents'* desires in the construction of the child's unconscious, as in Laplanche's concept of the 'enigmatic signifier'.[11] However, amongst contemporary psychoanalysts it is Jessica Benjamin who offers the most accessible critique of the narrowness of Oedipal thinking. Benjamin sees the Oedipus complex as representing too easy an acceptance of traditional dichotomising notions such as that the father is the primary symbol of reality and maturity, while the mother's pull is always to fantasy and narcissism. As she notes in her major work on domination, *The Bonds of Love*, versions of the Oedipus complex which draw on this 'Oedipus versus Narcissus' mentality in which the father 'liberates' the child from the regressive pull of dependency and incest, produce misogynistic and lifeless accounts of the possible arrangements of masculinity and femininity, based firmly around idealisation and denigration.

Paradoxically, the image of the liberating father undermines the acceptance of difference that the Oedipus complex is meant to embody. For the idea of the father as protection against 'limitless narcissism' at once authorises his idealisation and the mother's denigration . . . Difference turns out to be governed by the code of domination.[12]

What has to be achieved, she argues, both in individual development and in psycho-political theory, is a capacity to sustain an identification with 'sameness in difference', a capacity to recognise the other's *otherness* yet also appreciate the other's subjectivity and worth. Benjamin implies that this is to be managed neither by a regression to the pre-Oedipal mother, rather characteristic of object relations theory and involving a denial of the sexualised nature of gender differentiation, nor by the traditional Freudian or Lacanian adherence to

---

[10] Reich, W. (1946) *The Mass Psychology of Fascism* Harmondsworth: Penguin; Deleuze, G. and Guattari, F. (1977) *Anti-Oedipus* New York: Viking

[11] Laplanche, J. (1999) *Essays on Otherness* London: Routledge

[12] Benjamin, J. (1988) *The Bonds of Love* London: Virago, 1990, p.135

the structuring power of the Oedipus situation, with its focus on lack and denial. Instead, she invokes both the pre-Oedipal, loving father, and a 'post-Oedipal' capacity to integrate the various identificatory positions which arise from the preceding developmental periods. The suggestion here is two fold. First, the father is not just limiting and repressive, as in the Oedipal story, but can in principle and frequently in reality also offer a loving identificatory figure to the young child. Boys and girls both identify with this loving father, just as they do with the powerful and loving mother. Secondly, 'dis-identification' is not an issue; rather, children make further – that is, multiple or 'polymorphous' – identifications with figures offering them things of value and thus creating the opportunity for more varied, less oppositional identity positions. That is, if things go well, there is no reason why the limitations on desire which characterise the Oedipus situation should be effectively the end of the developmental story. Rather, Benjamin claims that there could be a more mature, post-Oedipal state of mind in which the various 'elements of identification' are brought together in a kind of creative and non-threatening tension.[13] It is only through the achievement of this kind of integrative complementarity that the idealisation-denigration split so characteristic of Oedipal thinking can be overcome, hence making it possible for gender, and identities in general, to become more complex and open to the impact of others.

In this material, Benjamin manages to develop a critique of psychoanalysis' (and society's) Oedipal vision (the idea that the paternal Law necessarily fixes gender identity for all time) without bolstering an alternative version of the same vision by idealising the pre-Oedipal relationship with the mother, as object relations theorists tend to do. Staying within the terms of psychoanalysis, Benjamin nevertheless shows how psychoanalysis' opposition of pre-Oedipal and Oedipal has been part of a wider social process of polarising gender. In so doing, she articulates a psychoanalytic theory to contest this polarising, dichotomising tendency, one based on fluid and multiple identifications cutting across traditional 'paternal' and 'maternal' positions. Although this approach has some difficulties, which have

---

[13] Benjamin, J. (1998) *Shadow of the Other: Intersubjectivity and Gender in Psychoanalysis* New York: Routledge, pp.69–70

been raised by many critics who are basically in sympathy with Benjamin's general project,[14] what is worth holding onto is the possibility of living creatively with difference rather than seeking rigidity and sameness, something which is supposed to be embodied in the Oedipus complex, but which is often lost in its working out.

[14] Butler, J. (2000) Longing for Recognition: Commentary on the Work of Jessica Benjamin *Studies in Gender and Sexuality 1*, 271–290

9 Interpretation

In popular versions of psychoanalysis and amongst analysts themselves, interpretation, the procedure by which an analyst communicates to a patient the unconscious meaning of his or her actions and words, is seen as lying at the heart of psychoanalytic activity. 'Psychoanalysis itself might be defined in terms of it,' write Laplanche and Pontalis, 'as the bringing out of the latent meaning of given material.'[1] At root, psychoanalysis is formulated as a discipline devoted to uncovering hidden meanings, reaching below the surface of action and consciousness to reveal the disturbing elements of unconscious life. With psychoanalysis defined in these terms, based on the concept of 'depth', interpretation is bound in one way or another to be a significant feature of its activity. This assumes, of course, that there really are such 'depths'; that is, the practice of interpretation hinges on the existence of something that needs to be brought out, meanings which are not necessarily obvious but which have to be put into some kind of context. Psychoanalysis asserts that this context is that of the unconscious, but alternatives are envisionable, for example that the correct interpretations should find social causes for behaviour (loosely, the Marxist account) or spiritual ones (a religious view).

Some very strong debate has surrounded all this. This debate occurs within psychoanalysis in terms of the best way to understand how interpretations might work and what the appropriate balance might be between interpretive and other (for example, supportive 'holding' or 'containing') activities on the part of the analyst. It also occurs outside psychoanalysis, where critics have claimed either (or both) that interpretations are really *suggestions*, ideas imposed by the analyst on material (that is, the analyst reads meaning *into*, rather than *out of* the

---

[1] Laplanche, J. and Pontalis, J.-B. (1973) *The Language of Psychoanalysis* London: Hogarth Press, p.227

patient's discourse), or that there is no way of establishing the veracity and accuracy of particular interpretations as they are applied in therapy (or anywhere else). Is interpretation *speculation*, a way of creating a plausible narrative out of essentially meaningless fragments, a 'seductive' game invented by psychoanalysis, or a set of rigorous procedures for establishing the wishes and impulses which 'really' motivate human concerns?

Sandler, Dare and Holder list a number of ways in which the term 'interpretation' has been used in the analytic literature: to refer to the analyst's inferences as to the meaning of the patient's communications; to refer to the analyst's articulation of those inferences; to refer only to verbal interventions which have the aim of bringing about 'dynamic change' through insight; or to refer to *all* comments by the analyst.[2] They also note that some analysts have rejected the notion of interpretation altogether, a point to be returned to later. After reviewing all these positions, Sandler *et al.* suggest a definition of interpretation as a communication from the analyst with a specific intended effect on the patient: 'all comments and other verbal interventions which have the aim of immediately making the patient aware of some aspect of his psychological functioning of which he was not previously conscious'.[3] This broad definition, which has the virtue of distinguishing between the analyst's *own* understanding of what is going on and what she or he communicates to the *patient*, has its roots in the idea that therapy operates by increasing the self-knowledge available to the patient. The argument is that this knowledge – known as 'insight' – will strengthen the ego and give it more power to control the unconscious impulses which are troubling it, or to tolerate the recognition of unconscious conflicts in consciousness, where they have a chance of being dealt with and resolved. Interpretation is therefore a key weapon in the analyst's armoury, the means by which this essential process of self-knowledge is sparked off.

In the classical psychoanalytic approach, interpretation is used cautiously and in a carefully, if informally, graded way. First comes a process of building up a 'working alliance' with the patient, so that the

---

[2] Sandler, J., Dare, C. and Holder, A. (1973) *The Patient and the Analyst* London: Maresfield Reprints, 1979

[3] Ibid., p.110

two protagonists in the analytic situation are felt to be, roughly speaking, on the same side, joined in a desire to support the patient's ego in its struggle for supremacy over the unconscious impulses which are troubling it. During this period, and at the various times in a therapy when the analyst might feel it necessary to retreat from too much confrontation into a supportive stance, interpretation will be used very sparingly, as the patient's ego is thought to be too fragile to deal with the consequences of a quick unravelling of the defences. For this is the principal focus of interpretations: demonstrating the activity of the defences so that the anxieties lying beneath them can be tracked; and subsequently exploring how these anxieties arise from specific unconscious conflicts. In the classical Freudian approach, the emphasis on balancing the intensity of interpretations against the capacity of the ego to cope with them entails proceeding in an order that reverses the developmental stages, from reasonably integrated genital concerns to more distorted and primitive anal and then oral ones. As defences, anxiety and emotions are interpreted at each level, the underlying conflicts which they reveal can be dealt with under the gaze of a gradually strengthened ego, freeing psychic energy and making it possible to move deeper. Gradually, as impulses at each level become more controllable, more basic conflicts are ready to be faced. In this process, the support offered by the analyst is a significant prop to the ego, allowing it to cope even with destructive emotions.

In line with their much greater emphasis on the interpersonal aspects of the analytic situation, many contemporary psychoanalysts, particularly those of the Kleinian school, are critical of the assumption embedded in the classical approach that interpretation is a matter of seeing material more 'realistically' than the patient can, and somehow explaining it. For many analysts, this underestimates the important impact that transference has on the proceedings; that is, the whole emotional power of interpretation resides in its contextualisation in a highly charged relationship, which in turn draws its energies not just from current concerns, but from repetition of the past. Where the Kleinian approach is most distinctive is in the content of these transference interpretations, which focus upon so-called 'primitive' material. This stance arises from two considerations. First, the Kleinian idea that transference operates through projective mechanisms which are basic to mental life and which are particularly characteristic defences in the formative and developmentally very early paranoid-schizoid period, leads to a concern with anxieties and splitting processes otherwise found in early infancy. Secondly, Kleinians argue that in order for unconscious material to be acceptable to consciousness, the anxiety that it generates has to be lessened *at the same time* as the defences are removed. This means, they claim, that interpretation of primitive unconscious contents and defences is crucial from the start of analysis. Hence, they place at least as much emphasis on the interpretation of anxieties as on the interpretation of defences, and do not follow the genital to anal to oral sequence marking gradually 'deeper' analytic work. Where classical analysts concentrate on interpretations which gradually uncover defences to allow careful exploration of the anxieties lying behind them, Kleinians are much more inclined to deal directly with the anxieties themselves, arguing that change does not come about through increased knowledge becoming available to the ego, which can then control conflicts more effectively, but through repairing splits at an unconscious level, aided by the internalisation of the analytic object. The value of interpretations, therefore, is that they feed back to the patient the projected elements in her or his personality, invested with the qualities of the analyst.

Other analysts have often criticised Kleinian work on a number of grounds: for example, that the emphasis on interpretation of primitive feelings often operates to the exclusion of anything else, including recognition of the occurrence of real events; or that the manner in which Kleinians launch into depth interpretations at the earliest possible moment can lead to overwhelming anxiety or the raising of destructive defences which cannot then be overcome. On the other hand, the emphasis amongst Kleinians on the intersubjective context for interpretation – that it takes place in a highly charged emotional setting and is thus different from, for example, seeing meaningful patterns in literary texts – is an important reminder that interpreting people might be a task of a different kind from other interpretive work.

How likely is it, however, that psychoanalytic interpretations are 'correct', and how might one ever know? There has been much debate on this issue, some of it surrounding a particularly thoughtful and provocative book by Adolf Grünbaum.[4] At the centre of his investigation stands a two-fold claim attributed to Freud: first, that accurate analytic interpretations are distinct from suggestions, but instead map out something which is 'true' of the patient; and secondly, that psychotherapeutic successes are produced by such accurate analytic interpretations. Grünbaum rather carefully examines the evidence bearing on both claims and finds it wanting. In particular, there are problems produced by what Freud calls suggestion and Grünbaum, with his eye on scientific method, calls 'contamination'. Given the setting of psychoanalysis, in which an intense, personal and unchaperoned encounter occurs between a person looking for help, self-knowledge and insight and an authoritative expert who is, in Lacan's eloquent phrase, 'supposed to know', how is it ever possible to be sure that the interpretations of the analyst are accurate? The crucial issue here is the set of phantasies cohering around the transference relationship, which itself is a testimony to the impossibility of seeing things 'as they are' in psychoanalysis, independently of any interpersonal mediation. That is, no reading of the 'truth' of the patient in analysis can ever be reliable, because every reading is a new construction, an interpersonal product, something arising out of the encounter between patient and analyst and invested with intense emotion and – if psychoanalysts themselves are right – unconscious phantasies.

Grünbaum takes this difficulty as fatal for Freud's claim that it is possible ever to know when one has spoken the truth about a patient. He acknowledges the sophistication of Freud's position here, for example in showing that Freud believed that an analyst could only legitimately override the stated objection of a patient to an interpretation if there were compelling additional evidence supporting the analyst's view. However, Grünbaum argues that all the information available to the psychoanalyst is in principle contaminated in the same way as is the patient's response: that is, what he terms Freud's appeal to 'consilience' (converging lines of independent evidence) must be spurious, because no data separate from what goes on between analyst and patient is allowed into the analytic setting. If the

---

[4] Grünbaum, A. (1984) *The Foundations of Psychoanalysis* Berkeley, CA: University of California Press

patient reports an occurrence which occurred outside the consulting room and which seems to support a line of analytic enquiry, he is still *reporting it* in the context of his relationship with the analyst, under the analyst's influence, as it were – perhaps to please or appease the analyst. Whatever occurs in the consulting room is created between analyst and patient; whether or not this should be called suggestion, it makes it impossible to distinguish between what is 'in' the patient and what is produced by the analytic process. The evidence which can be used by an analyst to support any particular claim concerning a patient simply does not lie about in a pure, 'uncontaminated' form: it always already shows signs of disturbance and reconstruction.

This line of argument has been quite compelling for many psycho-analysts as well as their critics, and has led to refinements in their views on how they might establish the accuracy – or at least the *helpfulness* – of particular interpretations. For example, many analysts have built on Freud's early idea that the analyst's activities should be 'directed only towards *facilitating* the patient's production of verbal material, in the belief that the stream of associations would eventually lead to the recall, more or less spontaneously, of emotionally charged memories surrounding important and significant events of the patient's past'.[5] The more up-to-date version of this is that the 'truth' of an interpreta-tion might be measured in terms of the patient's *response*, not specifically that they should agree with it, but rather that it should produce something new, some deepening of affect or empathy, or some productive line of thinking. For example, 'The validation of an interpretation . . . requires the emergence of new information in the patient's free associations, thus broadening and deepening the under-standing of a certain conflict; . . . a change in the patient's transference relationship or in his/her internal relationship to an extra-analytic object; and a rapprochement between the patient's experience and the analyst's understanding of it.'[6] Similarly, many 'hermeneutically' ori-ented psychoanalysts emphasise the 'performative' nature of inter-pretations: their value is in their effects, not necessarily in their

5 Sandler, J., Dare, C. and Holder, A. (1973) *The Patient and the Analyst* London: Maresfield Reprints, 1979, p.105
6 Kernberg, O. (1994) Validation in the Clinical Process *International Journal of Psycho-Analysis 75*, 1193–1200; pp.1195–1196

truthfulness, which indeed is impossible to separate out from the context of the specific relationship emerging in any particular patient and analyst pair. The implication of this approach for the status of interpretations is quite dramatic: 'the meaning of the material is highly dependent on who is listening to it, and . . . what was true for the treating analyst, at a particular time and place in the treatment, will never be true again.'[7]

The relativity of the notion of truth being worked with here certainly frees psychoanalysis from the untenable position of making claims to absolute knowledge, but it also raises considerable problems of its own. The most obvious of these is the question of what criteria are available for distinguishing between all the possible 'provisional truths' which might arise at any 'particular time and place' – including all the provisional or perhaps absolute falsehoods. Can any tale told by a psychoanalyst be believed? At least Freud tried to suggest the kind of things which might be regarded as evidence; can the more relativistic or agnostic critics salvage the value of interpretations by suggesting ways of regulating the freedom to imagine all sorts of impossible things – a freedom which sometimes seems very attractive to psychoanalysts, as well as to their patients?

The answer coming from advocates of this kind of position is that the sort of truth available in psychoanalysis is 'narrative truth'. The model for this in the first instance is the reading of literary texts: what is it that makes a text meaningful, that gives it conviction and sets it up as something significant and trustworthy even when one knows that it is actually absolute fiction? In general, answers to this question are usually given in terms of a variety of attributes of a text, such as its richness or coherence, measured for example by its capacity to articulate half-understood meanings, evoke emotions and throw light on obscurity. Reading a text interpretively is then a process of hunting for these meanings which, whether intended by the author or not, lie 'under' its surface. This is not an arbitrary process: it is quite possible to make interpretations of a text which have no coherence at all, and which fail to communicate anything; these would be failed, 'false' interpretations. But the search for narrative truth is extremely difficult, not only because there is a strong element of relativity brought into the situation by the variety of different narratives which might be available at any one time, but also because as the context for interpretation shifts – as culture changes, for example – so do the narratives which take hold and which hold conviction. Additionally, because psychoanalysis is not dealing with 'lifeless' texts but with living, reflexive beings, interpretations can be said to be coherent when they *offer* meanings to the patient, hence allowing something to change, something freeing or 'emancipatory' to occur.[8] What this might mean is that, eventually, the patient is indeed led to a form of linguistically mediated self-knowledge which gives her or him more control over experience, as psychoanalysts would hope, but this could have been produced by the compelling persuasive power of the analytic narrative rather than by the naming of a pre-existing unconscious state. That is, because so many of us understand ourselves in Freudian terms (unconscious, repression, trauma and the like) a well-structured psychoanalytic narrative is a powerful organiser of experience, bringing relief from the unsettledness of psychic turmoil; but it is still a form of suggestion, and some other compelling narrative (for example, a religious or social one, as mentioned above) might do equally well.

Does this matter? In many respects, the idea that the patient's response should decide the value of the analytic story has some attractive features. It offers a way of rooting theory in what actually takes place in the clinical situation, and – assuming the good faith of both analyst and patient – suggests that psychoanalysis is a collaborative enterprise aiming at constructing meanings which have emotional as well as intellectual force. In this regard it is close to many working psychoanalysts' accounts of the way they test the value of an interpretation: they tend to suggest that a good interpretation will bring on richer associational material, a change in the patient's emotional state, and alterations in the relationship with the analyst. On the other hand, most psychoanalysts would also argue that there may be perfectly good interpretations which pass patients by or are actively refuted by them, because their truth lies in the complex of negative

[8] Habermas, J. (1975) *Knowledge and Human Interests* London: Heinemann

personal attributes and feeling states to which they draw attention. But the key issue is again that it is not necessarily the case that just because an interpretation has an *effect*, it is actually *true*. As noted above, a compelling story might simply be powerfully persuasive – the recent disputes over 'recovered memory' attest to this, in which it seems that memories which are, to the extent one can be sure, untrue can at times be produced in confirmation of certain therapeutic suggestions.[9] More generally, people can often be sparked off by something someone says, producing changes in their lives whether or not they believe the original statement was true. Similarly, that a patient is able to make use of an interpretation is in no way a direct test of its veracity; it might simply attest to the power of the analytic situation.

We are left at the moment with an understanding that interpretation is a central theoretical notion in psychoanalysis, based on the assumption that there is a 'depth' underneath the 'surface' of people's lives, and that it is also a central element in the psychoanalyst's technical armoury. However, how one works out whether an interpretation is a 'good' or 'bad' one, let alone' true' or 'false' is deeply problematic. In addition, there is also a strand of psychoanalytic thinking which is antagonistic to giving interpretation such a major role. Long ago, Karl Menninger commented, 'Interpretation is a rather presumptuous term . . . I dislike the word because it gives young analysts the wrong idea about their main function. They need to be reminded that they are not oracles, not wizards, not linguists, not detectives, not great wise men who, like Joseph and Daniel, "interpret" dreams – but quiet observers, listeners, and occasionally commentators. . . . their *occasional* active participation is better called intervention. It may or may not "interpret" something. It may or may not be an interruption. But whenever the analyst speaks he contributes to a process.'[10]

Jacques Lacan, too, was deeply critical of analysts who seemed too keen to take up the position of 'the subject supposed to know' and behave as if they actually did know anything. The consequence, he thought, was not just analytic arrogance but the reduction of analysis

---

[9] This does not mean that all such memories are 'false'. See Prager, J. (1998) *Presenting the Past: Psychoanalysis and the Sociology of Misremembering* Cambridge, Mass.: Harvard

[10] Menninger, K. (1958) *Theory of Psychoanalytic Technique* New York: Basic Books

to a game in which patients could predict easily what an analyst might say – hence producing the phenomenon in which Freudian patients have Freudian dreams, Kleinian ones Kleinian dreams, and so on. What is critical in psychoanalysis is to hold on to the specificity of each person's discourse; by its very nature this means that it cannot be 'interpreted' in the light of any pre-existing scheme, but can only be negotiated. This is why, as Evans notes, Lacan argued that analytic interpretations 'should no longer aim at discovering a hidden meaning, but rather at disrupting meaning'; that is, 'far from offering the analysand a new message, the interpretation should serve merely to enable the analysand to hear the message he is unconsciously addressing to himself ... The analyst plays on the ambiguity of the analysand's speech, bringing out its multiple meanings.'[11] For the Lacanians, as for the early Freud, the point of an interpretation is to facilitate the patient's speech. In particular, the analyst *interrupts* when this speech has become too predictable and geared to avoiding unconscious material, and comments in ways which aim to promote the flow of free associations, without ever believing that these comments represent the truth. Seen in this way, it is for the patient to interpret, not the analyst.

[11] Evans, D. (1996) *An Introductory Dictionary of Lacanian Psychoanalysis* London: Routledge, p.89

10 Resistance

WHEREAS the term *defensive* applies in general to the behaviour and states of mind of people who cannot face up to some 'truth' about themselves, psychoanalysis retains a differentiation between the way in which this manifests itself in everyday life, and what happens in the psychoanalytic situation. The defences operate all the time, in order to protect the ego against the full force of unconscious wishes; but it is only in psychoanalysis that one observes the workings of *resistance*, this being a term referring specifically to a patient's opposition to progress. In particular, it denotes the patient's ambivalence, whereby she or he might be genuinely seeking therapeutic help yet might also be undermining all attempts to achieve insight into the unconscious source or meaning of the symptoms which have been causing trouble – hence subverting the therapeutic process. Resistance, therefore, has general significance as a way of indicating how a person might want something (for example, to change) but not want it at the same time.

What exactly is resistance *resistance to*? Although it is unconscious material that is defended against, the actual procedure to which the patient objects is what is termed the 'fundamental rule' of psycho-analysis, the command to free associate. That is, resistance is an observable phenomenon, couched in terms of a refusal to keep to the rules of the game, even after they have been accepted. This refusal, fur-thermore, is an inevitable and integral part of the psychoanalytic process. The 'fundamental rule' of analysis is that the patient relin-quishes her or his power to censor thoughts and, instead, 'free asso-ciates', saying everything that comes into her or his mind, however apparently trivial or embarrassing. But such relinquishing of censor-ship is never actually possible: Freud avers that in every instance free association breaks down, and it is precisely at that point that the ana-lyst knows that significant material is to be found. The patient agrees to the rule, but still tries to maintain some places of asylum within the mind, because of the preciousness of the secret knowledge available to her or himself and the threatening consequences to the defences if it should come to light. In a telling analogy, Freud locates the hidden impulse that provokes this anxiety in the realms of criminality.

Suppose that in a town like Vienna the experiment was made of treating a square such as the Hohe Markt, or a church like St. Stephen's, as places where no arrests might be made, and suppose we then wanted to catch a particular criminal. We could be quite sure of finding him in the sanctuary.[1]

The deep causes of unrest are hiding somewhere, and it would indeed be remarkable if the patient could locate them by a simple act of free speech. Hence, although the psychoanalyst purports to be listening to the talk of the patient, what are actually at the centre of analytic attention are the moments when talk is blocked, the slips and silences that infiltrate the patient's associations and which might be leverage points to begin the process of shifting the great mass of resistance. This is unlikely to be an easy process, and the obstacles to progress are very many, ranging from initial resistances which can only be dealt with by gradually winning the trust of the patient, to all the 'chance events' that occur in a person's life which can be made into reasons for interfering with or breaking off the analysis. The symptoms are, after all, serving a purpose, and there is a considerable amount of pain involved in giving them up.

The particular value of resistance for psychoanalysis, therefore, consists in the fact that when the analyst comes up against the patient's refusal to indulge in free association, it is an indication that important material is present which requires attention. Resistance is consequently not only an obstacle to analytic progress but also an indication of the areas requiring most careful and thorough interpretation. As Freud developed his ideas, he came to see the identification of repressed material through observation of resistance as the crucial first stage in analysing the repressions. The hiding place of repressed material is given away by what happens in analysis, by how the patient goes quiet at certain points, denies the significance of things she or he

[1] Freud, S. (1917) *Introductory Lectures on Psychoanalysis* Harmondsworth: Penguin, 1974, p.329

does, refuses to accept the analyst's interpretations, or messes around with the analytic boundaries (for example by missing or appearing late to sessions). It also appears in the transference, as the powerful emotions generated by the relational aspects of the analytic encounter themselves inhibit the work of unravelling the defences and exploring the anxieties and unconscious wishes lying behind them.

Although resistance was primarily formulated by Freud as whatever inhibits free association, its growing significance as a spur to therapeutic work led him to differentiate between a number of different types, or at least sources, of resistance – a differentiation which has remained influential amongst analysts.[2] Three of these types are activities of the ego, aimed at stopping it experiencing the discomfort of unconscious material breaking through. The purest of these is 'repression-resistance', which is provoked by free association and which grows in strength as the repressed comes closer to the surface, as a kind of increasingly desperate warding-off manoeuvre. The second ego resistance is 'transference-resistance' which 'has the special quality that it both expresses, and reflects the struggle against, infantile impulses which have emerged, in direct or modified form, in relation to the person of the analyst.'[3] The third resistance is in the form of a clinging onto 'secondary gain', that is, the benefits that the symptoms have provided for the patient, for example in allowing her or him to avoid challenging situations, or to obtain sympathy and support from other people. The next Freudian resistance is unconscious or 'id-resistance', which is manifested in the form of the 'compulsion to repeat', thought of by Freud as the conservative tendency of the unconscious to keep insisting on ancient patterns of drive release, culminating in the idea that what always repeats is death. For psychoanalysts, this tendency of the unconscious to find its way back into old paths is a major reason why resistance never ends, and why 'working through' – the laborious, repetitive task of going over and over the same things as they appear in new ways – is essential to psychoanalysis. Finally in the list of resistances is that arising from the operation of the superego, the 'part' of the mind in which guilt is held, and which is constantly appealing for

---

[2] Sandler, J., Dare, C. and Holder, A. (1973) *The Patient and the Analyst* London: Maresfield Reprints, 1979

[3] Ibid., pp.74–5

punishment. This is a source of one weird reality of psychoanalytic progress: that patients can come seeking help, but then reject it when it is offered, because they do not feel they deserve it.

The basic structure of the theory of resistance as laid down by Freud has proved quite robust, although there are a variety of different emphases to be found in the work, for example, of Kleinians (who focus their attention on how resistance appears in the negative transference, the complex of hostile feelings directed by the patient towards the analyst) and Lacanians (who see resistance as aspects of the ego acting as a kind of deception or 'lure' which the analyst is best to ignore, as it blocks the route to acknowledging unconscious desire). What is worth considering briefly, however, is the question of whether resistance is genuinely an irreducible aspect of the psychoanalytic situation, as most analysts assert, or whether it is in part or whole a product of the analyst's activity. Donald Winnicott, for example, produced a new attitude in his account of the 'management' of schizoid or 'borderline' patients, by arguing that their resistances should not be analysed as aspects of the patient's pathology, as they would be with neurotics. Instead, with schizoid patients the resistance must be viewed as a sign that *the analyst* has made a mistake, and must allow acknowledgement of the reality of that error, so that the patient can experience realistic anger in the context of a relationship that continues to be secure. If the analyst defends her or himself, 'the patient misses the opportunity for being angry about a past failure just where anger was becoming possible for the first time'.[4] The negative transference of Kleinian analysis is thus replaced by objective anger about the analyst's failures; expression of this anger within the safety of the carefully managed setting allows integration of the self to begin to occur. The wider point here is of how to distinguish, in the psychoanalytic situation as elsewhere, between what blocks progress in the patient and what blocks it in the analyst. The usual psychoanalytic stance is to 'blame' the patient, seeing the obstacles to therapy as arising from her or his investment in staying the same; but one has to ask, what about the weak, incompetent or misguided analyst who simply gets it wrong?

[4] Winnicott, D. (1958) *Through Paediatrics to Psychoanalysis* London: Hogarth Press, 1958, p.298

11   Transference

WHILE psychoanalysis started off as an investigative activity, in which the main purpose of treatment was to lift repression through interpretation, the mechanism of therapy receiving most attention nowadays is that of transference. This is in some ways a peculiar phenomenon, referring to the various ways in which the past returns in the present of the analytic encounter. What are 'transferred' here are feelings which properly belong elsewhere, usually attached in some way to persons or situations of long ago, and never fully dealt with. In the more radical language of the Kleinians, however, it is parts of the self that are transferred from the patient to the analyst, an idea which in many ways has revolutionised the theory and practice of psychoanalytic psychotherapy.

In Freud's thought and in that of the 'classical Freudians', transference is understood to be based on the psychological mechanism of displacement: a set of intense feelings is diverted from the person to whom they belong and instead is directed towards some other person, in this instance the psychoanalyst. Freud's first systematic formulation of transference, in the 'Dora' case study of 1905, stresses the way such transferences represent, but are not in fact the same as, the unconscious complexes from which they arise. Transferences are,

new editions or facsimiles of the impulses and phantasies which are aroused during the progress of the analysis; but they have this peculiarity, which is characteristic of their species, that they replace some earlier person by the person of the physician. To put it another way: a whole series of psychological experiences are revived, not as belonging to the past, but as applying to the person of the physician at the present moment.[1]

---

[1] Freud, S. (1905) Fragment of an analysis of a case of hysteria. In S. Freud, *Case Histories* Harmondsworth: Penguin, 1977; pp.157–8

One of the striking elements in this definition is the idea of a 'new edition' and the imagery of *rewriting*: some basic 'ur-text', usually a set of feelings towards a parent, is the original and true source of the peculiar story told in the analytic situation. Importantly, this means that the psychoanalytic encounter can only be understood in the light of this ur-text: there is not enough in the surface exchanges between analyst and patient to justify the intensity of the patient's feelings unless it is understood that the analytic situation functions as a kind of trigger for the emergence of some passion which was already there. This is experienced as a new feeling, but in reality it is a recapitulation, a facsimile, a copy taken for the original. It is,

a *specific illusion* which develops in regard to the other person, one which, unbeknown to the subject, represents, in some of its features, a repetition of a relationship towards an important figure in the person's past.[2]

One of the key notions in this definition is contained in the phrase 'unbeknown to the subject'. The strong argument here, maintained through all the developments in the theory of transference which have occurred during the last fifty years, is that one might be aware of very intense emotions when in a relationship with another person, without recognising the source and hence the original and continuing meaning of those emotions. These unconscious feelings from the past dictate irrational responses to the present; indeed, this is what betrays them as transference feelings – that their fervour is out of line with what the situation demands. This explains the otherwise ridiculous phenomenon of love at first sight, as well as unwarranted hatred for someone whom one barely knows; it is also a source of the enormous passion (both positive and negative) which many people show towards the institutions of which they are part – including the institutions of psychoanalysis ('psychoanalysis is powerfully addictive, and "transference" is the name, though not in any serious sense the explanation, of this phenomenon'[3]). Most importantly, it is the reason why psychoanalysis is a significant experience, more than it might be if all that happened therein was that a patient went to talk to some kind of doctor.

[2] Sandler, J., Dare, C. and Holder, A. (1973) *The Patient and the Analyst* London: Maresfield, p.47

[3] Gellner, E. (1985) *The Psychoanalytic Movement* London: Paladin; p.55

At its broadest, as indicated above, the concept of transference refers to a process which is prevalent in everyday life and is not limited to the special circumstances of the analytic treatment situation. The basic idea is that our earliest relationships lay down inside us general tendencies towards certain ways of relating, repeated in all our interactions with other people. We deal with others not just in terms of their 'reality', but in line with unconscious expectations and phantasies of our own. This is a normal process, bringing about normal difficulties and distortions ('misrecognitions') which can become pathological under certain circumstances – and often does in marriages or in the cut and thrust of family or working life. Much of life seems to consist in negotiating between our preconceptions of others and the experiences we actually allow ourselves to have of them, and many people seem to have difficulty in holding off from judgement long enough to allow themselves to be surprised. Furthermore, transference is an escalating phenomenon: once the self imposes it on the other, it tends to create its own reality, so that the other comes to act in line with what the self expects. For example, one major difficulty in any authority relationship, such as teaching or managing others, is to deal with the transferences of those one has authority over; very often, these transferences are so strong and stereotyped they can make anyone who is not exceptionally independently-minded into a kind of parody of the other's unspoken expectations. What makes transferences more than just prejudices is, of course, that they are *unconscious*: this is why they have such power and are so difficult to identify and change.

Although all this is generally applicable, it is in the context of the relationship with the analyst that transference really comes into its own. From the moment the patient meets the analyst, transference is present, operating initially to oppose progress but gradually taking on the dual role of resistance and expression of the patient's personal history. That is, the patient's transference response to the analyst not only facilitates (in the case of a positive, loving transference) or inhibits (negative, oppositional transference) the therapy; it is *symptomatic* of the patient's unconscious phantasies about relationships and hence indicative of conflicts which the analysis will need to address. Thus, Freud argues that although transference is experienced by the patient as real and as referring to the person of the analyst, it actually has nothing to do with current interactions but is totally a reconstruction of infantile feelings, hence usefully revealing to the analyst the 'kernel of [the patient's] intimate life history'.[4] This allows a curious 'as if' quality to infiltrate the analytic session: the patient behaves as if her or his feelings were legitimately directed towards the analyst, while the latter interprets them as displacements, whose appropriate objects belong to the past. The analyst must be particularly on guard against acting in accord with the patient's transference and hence muddling up the patient's phantasies about the analyst with what happens in reality; this will confuse the patient, encourage infantile dependence and a retreat from the real world, and also support the patient's resistances as she or he will not have to face up to the actual limits that analysis places on the satisfaction of desire. Transference, at least for Freud, is thus an intense set of feelings experienced by one partner in the therapeutic encounter, but kept at a distance and interpreted by the other.

There are three things which distinguish the treatment of transference in the analytic situation from others. First, transference is encouraged by the structure of analysis, the dependency it generates and the withdrawal of the analyst from full presence; this prevents the kind of reality-testing which occurs in ordinary life and which enables people to modify their experiences of one another. By being no-one, it is commonly asserted, the analyst can become anyone in the patient's imagination. Secondly, the behaviour of the analyst is different from that of people in ordinary settings. Not only is the analyst passive and obscure, refusing to reveal anything of her or himself and yet expecting the patient to talk in detail about the most personal and embarrassing concerns, but she or he actively comments on the transference, drawing the patient's attention to it and assertively trying to work out what meaning it has. This is what gives power to the interpretations which the analyst uses: they take place in the context of a highly charged relationship, which draws its energy not just from current concerns, but from repetition of the past. Any statement of analyst to

---

[4] Freud, S. (1926) The Question of Lay Analysis. In S. Freud *Two Short Accounts of Psychoanalysis* Harmondsworth: Penguin, 1962, p.141

patient is read through the mists of transference, so that it can some-times even be converted into its opposite; the patient's response is then taken up and reinterpreted, a looking-glass regress forcing realignment of psychic material. This makes interpretation deeply problematic, as one can never be sure how any particular statement of analyst to patient will be heard, and hence of what it might come to mean. On the other hand, it is because of transference – the stirring up of intense unconscious emotions by the analytic situation – that inter-pretations have any force at all.

A third distinctive characteristic of the analytic situation, according to Freud, resides in a special kind of transference that occurs in ther-apy, the 'transference neurosis', in which 'all the patient's symptoms have abandoned their original meaning and have taken on a new sense which lies in a relation to the transference.'[5] An 'artificial neurosis' is created which not only mimics the real illness, making it visible to the analyst and hence susceptible to her or his interpretations, but also attracts energy away from the original symptoms. This is already an advance, because the various unreal objects to which psychological energy had been attached, generating anxieties of various kinds, now become unified into one, albeit still unreal, object – the analyst. With the articulation of the neurosis in the consulting room, the analyst is able to engage with it directly, making focused interpretations and allowing unconscious conflicts to be examined and (hopefully) resolved without provoking too much damage in the patient's outside life. Finally, at the end of therapy the transference neurosis is dissolved and the energy invested in the 'temporary object', the analyst, is returned to the disposal of the ego. This whole process is particularly facilitated by the way the analyst sides with the patient's ego, making it stronger and hence more ready to give some licence to libidinal impulses without having to resort to the extreme defences that were previously used.

In their essay on transference, Sandler *et al*[6] note that the term has expanded widely since Freud's time, and list five different uses which

[5] Freud, S. (1917) *Introductory Lectures on Psychoanalysis* Harmondsworth: Penguin, 1974, p.496

[6] Sandler, J., Dare, C. and Holder, A. (1973) *The Patient and the Analyst* London: Maresfield Reprints, 1979

have become widespread. One of these is the Freudian idea of denoting 'the emergence of infantile feelings and attitudes in a new form, directed towards the person of the analyst'; another is closely related, 'to encompass all "inappropriate" thoughts, attitudes, fantasies and emotions which are revivals of the past and which the patient may display (whether he is conscious of them or not) in relation to the analyst.' What is noticeable about both these loosely Freudian understandings is that they posit a reasonably clear differentiation between the 'irrationality' of transference and the rationality of the analyst and of the ordinary world. That is, they assume that the task of distinguishing between transference and non-transference phenomena – between realistic and distorted perceptions – is a manageable one.

Some analysts argue, however, that this is never as easy as it seems, that the consulting room is full to the brim with phantasy material and, because of the workings of the unconscious and of the transference phenomena through which it speaks, there is no possibility of clearly separating truth from illusion. For them, transference refers to '*all* aspects of the patient's relationship to his analyst. . . . Indeed, *every* verbal and non-verbal communication or expression by the patient during the course of his analysis is regarded as transference. Analysts who take this view of transference regard all the patient's associations as essentially referring to some thought or feeling about the analyst.'[7] This is the approach adopted above all by the Kleinian school of psychoanalysis. Arising out of the practical considerations of her work with children and the theoretical implications of her understanding of the ubiquity of unconscious phantasy, transference came to be understood by Klein as a process in which *current* emotions and parts of the self were externalised (projected) into the relationship with the analyst, in order primarily to deal with anxiety, but also enabling therapeutic activity to occur.

The practice of Kleinian psychoanalysis has become an understanding of the transference as an expression of unconscious phantasy, active right here and now in the moment of the analysis.[8]

---

[7] Ibid, p.46
[8] Hinshelwood, R. (1991) *A Dictionary of Kleinian Thought* London: Free Association Books, p.465

This does not mean that Kleinians ignore the historical dimension of transference activity. For one thing, Klein stated explicitly that the mechanisms on which transference is based are fundamental aspects of human mental functioning which themselves have origins in infantile psychological processing – projection, paranoid schizoid functioning, projective identification and so on. Klein states, 'I hold that transference originates in the same processes which in the earliest stages determine object relations.'[9] Just as the infant projects into the mother's breast her or his terrifying destructive phantasies, so does the patient use the analyst as a receptacle for split off feelings and bits of the self. Moreover, Kleinian technique also stresses a historical, developmental dimension in the interpretive process, which seeks to examine the connections between the current transference feelings and past relationships. However, what becomes apparent in the Kleinian mode of understanding and working with the transference, is that the Freudian conceptualisation of the transference as a kind of irrational error, a misreading of the present in terms of the past, gives way to a more fluid and fertile understanding in which current emotions and self-representations, infused of course by past experiences but nevertheless alive and growing *now*, take precedence. Seen in this way, transference becomes an expression of the impregnation of the analytic relationship with phantasy and desire, with the imaginative flux that constitutes human subjectivity.

The differing definitions of transference relate to some important differences in accounts of the mechanism by which transference operates. In the classical view, as noted above, transference is a form of *displacement*: feelings that properly belong in one relationship, directed towards some particular person or persons, instead become concentrated on to the analyst. Because this assumes the possibility of forming relatively coherent relationships, classical theory makes transference the product of a fairly late period in the child's life, when the ego is well developed and there is a clearly established sense of self and of the boundary between self and others. The therapeutic focus is on an autonomous individual psyche which has become fixated in

[9] Klein, M. (1952) The origins of transference. In M. Klein, *Envy and Gratitude and Other Works* New York: Delta, p.53

certain ways, but which is basically capable of forming relationships and of distinguishing between fantasy and reality – hence the reluctance of classical analysts to treat psychotics, who supposedly lack these capabilities. The analyst's task is to improve the patient's capacity to see the world realistically by pointing out what happens in the transference, thus helping the patient see how her or his various phantasies are distorting contemporary relationships. The analyst in this scenario is in many respects outside the interaction: the passive recipient of, or 'sounding board' for, the patient's impulses and phantasies, relatively unaffected by them but commenting upon them in order to clarify their sense. Hence, the analyst's *refusal* to accept the imaginary role given to her or him by the patient is seen as one of the major techniques for revealing repressed material; analysis is a paradoxically intense practice of non-engagement.

In the classical view, therefore, the analyst functions as a mirror *onto* which the patient displaces her or his impulses. In contrast, Kleinians describe the analyst as a receptacle *into* which internal figures and the feelings that surround them are projected. The crucial word here is 'projection', especially as it is linked with the reformulation of developmental theory by Klein which makes projection and introjection into basic mental processes. Because, Kleinians believe, phantasy is always in operation and there is no pure area of 'realistic' perception free from it, and because projection is so pervasive that these 'internal' phantasies are always being put out into external objects, then it is impossible to differentiate clearly between transference and non-transference phenomena in analysis. Anything that happens will be infused with the patient's projections; transference is everywhere. Hanna Segal formulates this by asserting that all aspects of the patient's communications in the session contain 'an element of unconscious phantasy', even if they appear to be concerned with external facts; this is 'equivalent to saying that all communications contain something relevant to the transference situation.'[10] Hence, Kleinian technique centres on the interpretation *as transference phenomena* of all the varied material produced by the patient.

---

[10] Segal, H. (1981) *The Work of Hanna Segal* New York: Jason Aronson, p.8

Another directive of Kleinian practice arises from their insistence on the destructive aspects of early life, leading to a focus on the *negative* transference, the complex of hostile feelings which the patient may bring to bear on the analyst. Klein argues that working through envious and destructive feelings in therapy is a necessary prerequisite for any integration of the personality; it is through the analysis of the negative transference that this comes about, something which again involves exploration of early destructive feelings.

We can fully appreciate the interconnections between positive and negative transferences only if we explore the early interplay between love and hate, and the vicious circle of aggression, anxieties, feelings of guilt and increased aggression, as well as the various aspects of objects towards whom these conflicting emotions and anxieties are directed.[11]

The fundamental task of analysis is to enable integration of the personality to occur through overcoming splits in the psyche which are perpetuated by unresolved primitive conflicts. The appropriate method is to analyse both sides of the early love-hate conflict as they are replayed in the positive and negative transference. Destructive and loving feelings can by this means gradually be brought together in the presence of introjection of the good analytic object, allowing splitting to be overcome and integration of the personality to begin. Especially, it will be essential for the patient to have the experience of projecting hostile feelings into the analyst and having them 'contained' therein, so that they can lose some of their sting and be given back, through the analyst's interpretation of the negative transference, in a more meaningful and less devastating form. Only thus will integration begin to occur. The analyst's task in this is essentially one of survival and of maintaining a capacity for non-retaliatory thoughtfulness, so that the supposedly destructive transference derived from early envious feelings can be brought under control.

It is apparent here that transference has been moved to the centre of the psychoanalytic process in a way never envisioned by Freud. Sandler and his colleagues note, 'The understanding and analysis of transference phenomena are regarded by psychoanalysts as being at the very

---

[11]   Klein, M. (1952) The Origins of Transference. In M. Klein, *Envy and Gratitude and Other Works* New York: Delta, p.53

centre of their therapeutic technique, and the concept is widely applied outside psychoanalysis in the attempt to understand human relationships in general.'[12] The logic here is very persuasive, as the psychoanalytic concern with unconscious phantasy becomes enacted in the technique of psychotherapy, focusing everything onto the relationship between analyst and patient as it emerges in all its complexity. Whether the process is understood to be one of teasing out irrational from rational thought, or utilising feelings to index and provoke unconscious change, transference is the special medium that the psychoanalytic encounter trades in. It is worth noting here, however, that there are some voices warning against this expansionist tendency. Sandler and his colleagues themselves want to limit the notion so that it does not apply to everything: 'It would seem to be useful,' they write, 'to differentiate transference from non-transference elements, rather than to label all elements in the relationship (arising from the side of the patient) as transference. This may lead to greater precision in defining the clinically important elements in a whole variety of situations and elucidating the relative roles of the many factors which enter into the interaction between patient and therapist in any form of treatment.'[13] However, this idea is once again based on the premise that it is possible to distinguish between the distorted view of reality held by the patient and the more accurate view held by the analyst, a situation rendered problematic by the existence of the unconscious itself. That is, what psychoanalysis shows us is that everything is shot through with unconscious phantasy, making disputable any claim to be able to see things clearly.

While the Kleinian assertion of the ubiquity of transference may be the most influential innovation since Freud, Jacques Lacan's understanding of the concept also presents a challenging and novel view which casts the psychoanalytic situation in a light significantly different from that thrown on it by most other analysts. The key idea here is that of the psychoanalyst in the transference as 'the subject supposed to know',[14] by which is meant that there is a common way of relating

---

[12] Sandler, J., Dare, C. and Holder, A. (1973) *The Patient and the Analyst* London: Maresfield Reprints, 1979, p.37

[13] Ibid., p.48

[14] Lacan, J. (1972–3) God and the *Jouissance* of The Woman. In J. Mitchell and J. Rose (eds) *Feminine Sexuality* London: Macmillan, 1982, p.139

to the analyst as if she or he possesses a particular knowledge or truth, and that part of the process of analysis is discovering that this is a fantasy – that no-one owns the kinds of truths we all look for. This is a notion which offers considerable leverage when challenging simplistic ideas of the purpose of therapy or aspirations towards 'cure'.

The analyst is often thought to know the secret meaning of the analysand's words, the significations of speech of which even the speaker is unaware. This supposition alone (the supposition that the analyst is the one who knows) causes otherwise insignificant details (chance gestures, ambiguous remarks) to acquire retroactively a special meaning for the patient who 'supposes'.[15]

The patient invests hope in the analyst, but not just that; what defines transference is an unconscious belief that the analyst holds the answers to the patient's question, that all that is wrong in the patient's life can be eased away by the analyst's words of wisdom. This, however, is in Lacanian terms an 'imaginary' state of mind: in fact, there is no such capacity residing in anyone, and a great deal of trouble is caused by thinking that there is. Hence, Lacan is opposed to all psychoanalytic versions of cure which either hold that the analyst does know the difference between real and unreal (the classical view) or can become a 'good object' inside the patient (roughly, the Kleinian and object relational view). Rather, the end point of the Lacanian transference, the point at which it is 'dissolved', comes when the patient realises not just that the analyst has no answers, but that *no-one* possesses the answer to the question of existence. The 'subject supposed to know' is only *supposed* to know because of the phantasies generated about authority and knowledge itself; what signifies the end of transference – and of analysis – is the discovery that we can only know our *questions*, that no-one can be master of the unconscious.

[15] Evans, D. (1996) *An Introductory Dictionary of Lacanian Psychoanalysis* London: Routledge, p.197

12 Countertransference

LIKE transference, countertransference is an everyday experience augmented in the analytic situation, but perhaps not so very different in kind from things that happen all the time. One way of thinking about it is to consider the feelings one might have in another's presence. Especially when these feelings seem inexplicably strong – for example, excessive hostility to someone whom one has never met before, or overwhelming tiredness in the presence of someone else – there must always be a suspicion that these feelings derive from one's own unconscious. If one is a psychoanalyst or psychotherapist and these feelings are experienced in the presence of a patient, the question becomes that of whether they are in some way unconscious responses to that patient. This could be either because the patient reminds the analyst of something unconscious and personal, so producing a kind of transference response in the analyst, or because something very specific about the patient has 'got into' the analyst and elicited a set of feelings (thus boredom or anger might be a very specific response to a patient's depression).

In these alternatives, some of the different ways of understanding the phenomenon of countertransference can be found. For Freud, holding to a view of the analyst as a beacon of reason in a sea of irrationality, countertransference was a term used to describe an interference in the analyst's thinking derived from her or his own unconscious phantasies; that is, it was a direct counterpart to the patient's transference. 'Counter-transference was seen as a sort of "resistance" in the psychoanalyst towards his patient, resistance due to the arousal of unconscious conflicts by what the patient says, does or represents to the analyst.'[1] These unconscious conflicts could prevent the analyst

---

[1] Sandler, J., Dare, C. and Holder, A. (1973) *The Patient and the Analyst* London: Maresfield Reprints, 1979, p.62

getting a clear view of the patient's troubles, and in particular might inhibit the separation of the patient's transference feelings from realistic aspects of the situation. The source of countertransference would then be unanalysed aspects of the analyst's own personality, and as such the task would be to reduce the effects of these unanalysed conflicts as far as humanly possible.

Thus if a psychoanalyst had not resolved problems connected with his own aggression, for example, he might need to placate his patient whenever he detected aggressive feelings or thoughts towards him in the patient. Similarly, if the analyst is threatened by his own unconscious homosexual feelings, he may be unable to detect any homosexual implications in the patient's material; or, indeed, he may react with undue irritation to homosexual thoughts or wishes in the patient, may sidetrack the patient on to another topic, etc. The 'counter' in counter-transference may thus indicate a reaction in the analyst which implies a parallel to the patient's transference (as in 'counterpart') as well as being a reaction to them (as in 'counteract').[2]

From the Freudian perspective, then, countertransference is a fantasy relationship born out of the 'baggage' carried by the analyst and hence interferes with the analytic task of introducing a rational appreciation of reality into a version of the world distorted by unconscious, irrational wishes. In terms of technique, the task of the analyst would be 'to reduce manifestations of counter-transference as far as possible by means of personal analysis so that the analytic situation may ideally be structured exclusively by the patient's transference.'[3] Interestingly, elements of this view survive in the object relational claim that a 'real' relationship between analyst and patient is to be aspired to, so that fantasies on both sides need to be punctured and removed. Winnicott, for example, is quoted as seeing countertransference as the analyst's 'neurotic features which *spoil the professional attitude* and disturb the course of the analytic process as determined by the patient.'[4] Kleinians, on the other hand, have been much clearer that counter-

[2] Sandler, J., Dare, C. and Holder, A. (1973) *The Patient and the Analyst* London: Maresfield Reprints, 1979, p.62

[3] Laplanche, J. and Pontalis, J.-B. (1973) *The Language of Psychoanalysis* London: Hogarth Press, p.93

[4] Quoted in Sandler, J., Dare, C. and Holder, A. (1973) *The Patient and the Analyst* London: Maresfield Reprints, 1979, p.64

transference is a specific mechanism of therapeutic activity – it is the analyst's guide to what is happening in the phantasy dimension of the therapy, and hence is the source of her or his understanding of the patient's emotional and unconscious state. The idea here is that the analyst has an unconscious reaction to the specific qualities of the patient, and that the analyst needs to cultivate the capacity to register, recognise and understand this reaction and use it as a *guide* to the patient's transference. Put simply, the patient has inserted (projected) something into the analyst, and it is the analyst's task to find this projected element and defuse it, in order to give it back to the patient in a safe, more contained and manageable form.

The clearest early formulation of this position can be found in some seminal work by Paula Heimann. Recognising that any specific patient will produce a response in the analyst peculiar to that patient, she argues that by

comparing the feelings roused in himself with the content of the patient's associations and the qualities of his mood and behaviour, the analyst has the means for checking whether he has understood or failed to understand his patient.[5]

Here, the argument is that the analyst will have feelings called up by the analytic process, that these will relate to the analyst's own state of mind but will also be connected to the patient's mental state, and that it is a possible and important analytic task to distinguish between these two sources of the analyst's response. Rather than emphasising the role of the analyst in offering interpretations based on an accurate perception of reality, Kleinians and those influenced by their thought stress the way in which the analyst becomes a 'container' for the patient's projected feelings and parts of her or his self and object world. The analyst is consequently involved in an interpersonal interaction that operates on several levels, including that of the interpenetration of the unconscious of one participant by that of the other. The difference between analyst and patient is not, therefore, that one has transference feelings and the other has not, but that the analyst has the emotional calibration to be able to use the feelings stirred up inside

[5] Heimann, P. (1960) Counter-transference *British Journal of Medical Psychology 33*, 9–15, p.10

her or him to understand the patient's internal world. Hence, therapy becomes a two-way process whereby the working out of transference and counter-transference go on together, the analyst's awareness of this operating benevolently to provide new introjects for the patient to use. The patient's projections – whether emotions or parts of the self – become the central sources of feeling, reflection and interpretation; what the analyst does with these, how she or he infuses them with parts of her or his own self, is thus crucial to the progress of the analysis. The technical concern of this work is,

> To allow oneself to be guided, in the actual *interpretation*, by one's own counter-transference reactions, which in this perspective are often not distinguished from emotions felt. The approach is based on the tenet that resonance 'from unconscious to unconscious' constitutes the only authentically psycho-analytic form of communication.[6]

Transference and countertransference impact constantly on one another as analyst and patient become entwined in a deeply intersubjective relationship. The fluid process of encounter is one which has a structure of 'not knowing': that is, each unconscious emanation is met with a response, itself partly unconscious; and each response feeds a new emanation.

This image of the interpersonal encounter embedded in the transference-countertransference cycle is very influential and can be found in some contemporary Freudian as well as Kleinian work. Its implication is that there is a mode of knowing that operates at the unconscious level and is perhaps acting outside of language – although this is a point of dispute between Lacanians and Kleinians, for example. Whether coded symbolically or not, this notion of countertransference suggests that there is an intimate link between patient and analyst centred on the capacity of the analyst to feel unconscious resonance with the patient. The analyst's task becomes that of acting as a receptacle for the patient's unconscious phantasy whilst remaining anchored in the analyst's own self, so as not to enact the patient's disorder. The analyst is both in and out of her or his self, connected to the patient yet never quite one with her or him. The analytic encounter

---

[6] Laplanche, J. and Pontalis, J.-B. (1973) *The Language of Psychoanalysis* London: Hogarth Press, p.93

itself has become more interactional: not just the analyst observing and making sense of the patient's unconscious life, but both partners to the analysis locked in an intersubjective embrace, in which each feels the other's feelings. The analyst picks up through the counter-transference what is happening hidden in the patient's mind; the patient is constantly monitoring the analyst for evidence of whether the parts of her or himself which have been projected into the analyst are being contained and cared for, or are creating panic. The whole outcome of analysis depends on this intersubjective embrace being a benevolent one.

Glossary of Additional Terms

containment a term used particularly in Kleinian and object relations psychoanalysis to refer to a process whereby projections or projective identifications emitted by one person are 'held' by the other. In infancy, it is the mother who has to contain the destructive impulses of her infant; in therapy it is the analyst who contains the patient's projections. Containment is essential for the development of trust in a non-persecutory environment as well as a capacity to own one's own envious feelings.

death drive Freud always assumed the existence of two major groups of drives opposed to one another and therefore causing unconscious conflict. In his early theory these were the 'sexual' and 'ego-preservative' drives, but with the reformulation of drive theory in his 1920 book, *Beyond the Pleasure Principle*, the opposition proposed was between 'life' and 'death' drives. The death drive was the name given to a basic tendency in the human to seek reduction of tension, effectively to return to an inorganic state of complete rest. In its externalised form, this can appear as aggression or destruction, a point taken up by Melanie Klein who sees in-born envy as the pure expression of the death drive in every infant. That is, for Klein destructiveness is a necessary part of the human condition.

depressive position a Kleinian term referring both to a developmental stage and to a state of mind or way of experiencing the world. Following on from, and to a considerable degree resolving, the paranoid schizoid position, the infant gradually manages to bring together and introject split feelings. This means that loving and destructive impulses are brought into relationship with one another, along with the 'good' and 'bad' objects to which they have given rise. The inner state of mind thus produced is one in which love and hate are connected and there is a realisation that objects are ambivalent, not just ideal or evil. Depressive emotions follow from this as the subject experiences the damage done to objects through her or his own destructive impulses as resulting in real loss. Because of the complexity of feelings and object relationships which characterises it, the depressive position is seen as an advance on the paranoid schizoid position.

displacement an unconscious process and defence mechanisms whereby an affect is directed towards a particular person or object instead of towards the object to which it 'properly' belongs. This can set up a chain of associations and is also a major mechanism at work in the formation of dreams and neuroses. According to Freudians, it also lies at the root of transference.

drive the biological source of psychological activity. Freud assumed the existence of two sets of drives, initially the sexual and ego preservative drives and later the life and death drives. These were seen as being in opposition to one another, creating the complex arrays of repression and conflict characteristic of the unconscious. Drives have a 'source' (the bodily part to which they are attached, for example 'oral' drives), an 'aim' (to reduce tension) and an 'object' (that entity which allows the aim to be achieved). Later psychoanalysts have disputed over the concept of drives, with Klein seeing it as central while other object relations theorists have argued that it is biologically reductionist and at odds with contemporary neurological as well as psychological knowledge.

ego that part of the mental apparatus in which consciousness and perception reside and which has the phenomenological status of a self. Freud's word for the ego was 'das Ich', the 'I'. However, as well as housing consciousness it also contains unconscious elements; these are the defence mechanisms whose role it is to police the boundaries of ego and id and to ensure that troubling unconscious material is kept repressed. According to Freud's later 'structural' theory, the ego arises from the id both as a regulating agency acting to assert the primacy of the reality principle (adaptation to the external world), and through the internalisation of lost objects. This is one source for object relations thinking, as the structure of the ego is seen as given by these internalised objects. Lacanian psychoanalysis questions the autonomy of the ego, seeing it as a 'misperception' based on the adoption of an external image (the 'mirror' of the other's gaze) as being the truth of oneself. Whereas many psychoanalysts (followers of 'ego psychology') have emphasised the importance of strengthening the ego so that it can deal with unconscious conflicts more successfully, Lacanians claim that this is an alienating method mistaking the problem for the cure.

envy in Kleinian psychoanalysis, the pure expression of the death drive. Envy is characterised as an attack on the object, based on inborn destructive urges which are expressed whenever 'goodness' is encountered. In early development envy forces a splitting defence to come into operation, otherwise the infant's ego would be swamped by her or his own unconscious destructiveness. Throughout life, envy continues to operate to spoil goodness and love. It is opposed by the tendency towards integration supported by a containing environment, which allows envy to be appeased and joined (in the depressive position) to gratitude.

Freudian slip or 'parapraxis', the well-known tendency to make 'accidental' errors of speech or action that turn out, on analysis, to have unconscious significance. One of Freud's major early psychoanalytic works, *The Psychopathology of Everyday Life*, was devoted to this phenomenon.

id 'das Es' or the 'It', the term given by Freud in 1923 to the area of the mind constituted as the home of the drives and hence of repressed unconscious material. The id is a powerhouse of dynamic activity, where all material is unconscious and functions according to the pleasure principle, giving rise to all the pressures and tensions of psychic life.

Imaginary in Lacanian analysis, this is the 'order' of experience characterised by the narcissistic relation with the image, in which the phantasy is that wholeness and integrity can be achieved. The Imaginary begins in the pre-Oedipal stage with the 'mirror phase', taken as a point of traumatic jubilation in which the infant seems to recognise itself as something integrated and to be relieved from the pressure of being subject to powerful, fragmenting drives. The Imaginary continues throughout life as a tendency to act as if wholeness is possible, recognisable for example in the belief that a perfect lover can be found, or that there might be a Utopian political state, or that the analyst might be able to give a full answer to the questions of existence.

infantile sexuality Freud's assumption was that the sexual drive is at work from the start of life, a biological force towards activity and sexual enjoyment. It takes various forms during development, initially being organised around the mouth (the oral stage), then the anus and then the genitals. At each stage, sexuality is organised differently but is still sexuality, still an expression of the sexual drive. Hence, there is no period in life in which the human subject is not sexual, and infants' 'sexual' feelings are properly deserving of that name.

insight the term given to the state aspired to as an effect of an interpretation, or even the outcome of psychoanalysis. Insight is a combination of a cognitive recognition of the reality of an unconscious conflict coupled with an emotional or 'affective' reorganisation of psychic life around this recognition. That is, intellectual knowledge is not enough; the new, insightful awareness has to be fully experienced (especially, in the transference) for it to count as *psychoanalytic* knowledge. This is likely to involve a lengthy period of 'working through' even after awareness is achieved.

intersubjectivity a term used to refer to the capacity to represent another person as a 'subject' in the sense of a centre of consciousness with whom one can hold a relationship of mutual recognition. Because it is concerned with unconscious knowledge of the other, it is more than just an *interpersonal* relationship.

introjection the converse of projection, and closely linked with identification, introjection is a process whereby what is 'outside' is taken into the subject and made part of her or his phantasy life. In psychoanalysis, it implies the hope that what will be introjected is the analyst's capacity to be a 'good object' – for example, to maintain a thoughtful, alive stance in the face of the patient's hostile projections.

life drive the converse of the death drive, consisting of the sexual and ego preservative drives, and all impulses towards elaboration, complexity, unification and enjoyment.

narcissism is a complex and widely used term in contemporary psychoanalysis, designating both a normal developmental phase ('primary narcissism', in which the child has no concept of anything outside itself) and a set of psychopathological phenomena. At its core is the notion of an investment of sexual energy in the self, but this does not necessarily mean that the self is powerful. In fact, what has made narcissism a useful concept for the exploration of cultural phenomena, is the idea that it is based on a *fragile* self, starved of love, which gives rise to a defensive manipulativeness in relation to other people, designed to avoid intimate, dependent relationships. In some current Western theory, narcissism is used as a metaphor for the state of society as a whole.

object that 'thing' in the eternal world which can bring about the satisfaction of the drive. The object is *contingent* in Freud's theory; that is, it is determined by the individual's personal history (what she or he finds satisfying) rather than by any absolutely necessary connection with the drive. However, as Freud's theory developed to encompass a sophisticated understanding of the Oedipus complex (in which relationships with particular objects – the mother and father – are crucial) and an understanding of the ego as constituted in part through the internalisation of lost objects, the ground was cleared for the more central role given to objects in later analytic work. For Klein and the object relations theorists, the mind is largely made up of internalised representations of object relationships. Early on, these are 'part objects', parts of the body (usually the penis or breast) which are related to as if they were persons. Later on (for Kleinians, in the depressive position), it becomes possible for the child to experience whole objects, not just because the perceptual apparatus has become more sophisticated, but also because the child is more emotionally capable of acknowledging the existence of ambivalence. Hence, whole objects can be made up of contradictory elements without losing their unity.

object relations theory a term quite loosely applied to indicate any approach which focuses on the relationships between the developing ego and the 'objects' (people or parts of people) with whom it comes into contact. This puts it in opposition to classical Freudian theory, in which human psychology is driven by the need to find an outlet for drives, and it is in order to do this successfully that relationships with others are formed. In object relations theory, this order of events is reversed, Freud's drives being replaced by an assumption that humans are fundamentally relationship-seeking creatures. In terms of original thinkers, it refers specifically to the work of Fairbairn, Guntrip and Winnicott. Klein also has strong object relations elements in her theory and is consequently often included in this school, but her heavy use of drive theory marks her out as distinct. Object relations theory, with its focus on the two-person, pre-Oedipal relationship, has made a particularly strong contribution in theorising the environmental conditions necessary to promote healthy psychological development.

paranoid schizoid position the first proper developmental 'position' in Kleinian theory, characteristic of early infantile and of psychotic states of mind. Klein assumes the existence from birth of a primitive ego which is threatened with destruction by the operations of the death drive. The anxiety produced by this threat causes the defence of projection to be activated. The death drive, or, rather, its phantasised (envious) derivatives, are projected into the object; simultaneously, split-off elements of the life drive are also projected for safekeeping. This results in an experience of the object (the breast) as itself split into bad and good entities. The ego has thus rid itself of an internal threat, but now experiences an external threat – the persecuting bad breast. This state of being persecuted by split-off elements which have their origin in internal impulses is the paranoid schizoid position.

pleasure principle in Freud's theory, psychic life is governed by the tendency, built into the drives, to seek release of tension. This is experienced as *pleasure*, so the principle by which the unconscious functions – the principle of the 'primary process' – is to pursue pleasure and avoid pain. This tendency is opposed by the reality principle.

preconscious ideas are ideas which are not in consciousness but are not actually repressed, and hence are available for use if required.

psychodynamic a general term for the operation of active unconscious forces which have to be repressed in order to keep them out of awareness. Loosely speaking, psychodynamic theories are all approaches which propose the existence of such unconscious forces even if the theories are not themselves specifically psychoanalytic. Gestalt Therapy, Group Analysis and Transactional Analysis would be examples of non-psychoanalytic psychodynamic approaches.

psychosexual stages in Freud's theory, the developmental stages through which a child moves, each characterised by different organisations of the sexual drive. These are, conventionally, the oral, anal, phallic and genital stages.

reaction formation a defence mechanism characterised by the unconscious adoption of behaviours or attitudes which are the opposite of a repressed wish, for example obsessional control as a way of dealing with the desire for sexual or aggressive excess.

Real This is the third Lacanian order, out of which the Imaginary and Symbolic emerge. The Real is that which cannot be put into words, that dissolution or abyss from which the subject flees into the arms of symbolisation. It is hence experienced as a threat, an unconscious awareness of dissolution.

reality principle the principle of mental functioning characteristic of the ego and hence of 'secondary processing'. The reality principle seeks to organise and regulate the flow of energy and hence to mitigate the pleasure principle so that it can achieve its aims in ways which are congruent with what the external, social world can tolerate. As such, the reality principle is attuned to rationality and to social order, but it also has an important ego-protective role.

regression in general, a term referring to the tendency to return (regress) to earlier stages of development. This can happen as a routine mode of phantasy (for example, in sleep or in the comfort of sexual love), or as psychopathology (extreme dependence, utilisation of 'primitive' defences, retreat into narcissism and omnipotent wishes). Regression can also be observed in the transference as evidenced in the analytic situation, as the patient explores deeply repressed primitive feelings. Some analysts have tolerated quite extreme regressive states in patients who do not seem able to make use of interpretive work. For example, Winnicott suggested that for some 'schizoid' patients regression might represent a normal healing process whereby an early 'failure situation' is returned to and repaired. Analysis with such patients would therefore not be so much a process of making links between current emotions or perceptions and past experiences, but rather of *reliving* the past, of encouraging the patient to accept the security of the analyst's reliable presence to release the hidden 'true self' or regressed ego that had never been allowed to live.

subject a term which, in psychoanalysis, is especially associated with the Lacanian approach (it was not used by Freud), where it replaces the 'self', the 'individual' and other such terms. Lacan's idea of the subject is a contradictory one, drawing on the linguistic notion of the subject of a sentence, the psychological notion of the individual human entity with agency and subjectivity, and the social/political notion of being 'subject to' something more extensive than oneself (for example, the law against incest). The full human subject is 'subject to' both culture and the unconscious, and therefore functions in the Symbolic order.

sublimation a defence mechanism which Freud thought of as the source of creativity. Sublimation works by converting sexual energy into something more socially acceptable, for example a work of art or a piece of socially valued intellectual work. This allows the potentially subversive sexual drive to achieve expression in ways which bring credit to the subject and pleasure in the social sphere. Other analysts have developed additional or alternative views on creativity; for example, Kleinians see it as a *reparative* process, a way of making good the damage felt to have been done to the loved object, and hence an advanced element in the depressive position. Sublimation can be seen as a 'limit concept' for psychoanalysis, in that it forces it into contact with social and historical institutions and values.

superego the third mental 'agency' invented by Freud in his 1923 book, *The Ego and the Id*, seen by Freud as one of the 'masters' to which the ego owes allegiance. The superego develops out of the Oedipus complex as the internalisation of the paternal prohibition on incest, accompanied by the aggression attributed by the child to the father plus the child's own (repressed) hatred of the father. Set up in this way, the superego becomes an internal judge, scrutinising wishes as well as actions and adopting primarily a punitive attitude towards these wishes. In addition, it encompasses the earlier ego ideal (although some analysts see the superego and ego ideal as separate), and hence contains aspirational phantasies as well as critical ones. Later analysts have disputed the dating of the superego, with Kleinians in particular asserting that evidence of its existence can be found in very early pre-Oedipal material.

Symbolic the Lacanian 'order' that lies in tension with the Imaginary, shattering its promise of wholeness. In the Symbolic, the infant is made a human, social subject by becoming 'subject to' the structures of language. These make communication possible and hence are enabling, but they are also *constraining*, forcing the subject to give up the phantasy that it might be possible to make reality bend to one's wishes. Instead, in order to speak, one must tolerate being regulated by a law that stands outside one, with rules which make social being possible. In addition, the Symbolic introduces a split into the subject: as 'I' speak, so something is separated off from 'me' to become alienated in language. For Lacan, the moment of entry to this order is the castration complex.